THE GREAT I AM

The Great I AM
God
Jesus Christ
Holy Spirit

DEBRA CRYER THOMPSON

Designed by Vince Pannullo

ISBN:979-8-35095-343-5

Contents

PART 2

"For unto us a child is born, unto us a son is given: and the govern-
ment shall be upon his shoulder: and his name shall be called Wonderful,
Counsellor,
The mighty God, The everlasting Father, The Prince of Peace"
(Isaiah 9:6 King James Version).

DEDICATION

I dedicate this book to those who will soon know that God is the Father, Jesus Christ is the Son, and the Holy Spirit is the absolute I AM. To Christians who know that God and Jesus Christ is the Mighty, *I AM* of humanity. To pastors and teachers around the world who toil day and night to preach the Gospel of Christ—your work is not in vain. To my friends and colleagues who waited months and then years for me to complete "The Great I AM." Thank you for tolerance, encouragement, and prayers. To my sisters: Linda Hunter and Barbara Jordan, thank you.

To my husband, Earl and our children, Rachel, Elizabeth, and Cory Thompson. To my son-in-law Lawrence Hamilton and my grandchildren Jasmine Danielle Thompson-Hamilton and Carter Earl Thompson-Hamilton--thank you for your circle of love, support, belief, and encouragement.

I dedicate "The Great I AM" to the spirit of my mother Idella Hunter, who is singing in heaven. Her love, guidance, and wisdom led me to believe that dreams can become a reality.

To those who know *"the Great I AM,"* continue to persevere and keep the faith.

I AM sent me to you...

I can do all things through Christ, which strengtheneth me. Philippians 4:13

INTRODUCTION

I first experienced the presence of my heavenly Father decades ago. At that time, I was an active member of the Pentecostal church, which is my Christian foundation. In my Christian walk, the Holy Spirit speaks to me daily, but some experiences are much more profound than others. However, each experience is sweeter than the day before. A few years ago, I had a moving spiritual experience, it was early one Saturday morning when God said to me, "*I AM, the Great I AM. Many say that I AM*, but do they really know *who*, I AM? You will tell the world that *I AM Great* in ways they have not yet imagined." After a few moments, God said the book is "The Great I AM." God told me where to locate the Lord's Prayer and Psalm 23 [The Lord's My Shepherd]. Also, He told me precisely where to place these prayers in the message. God spoke no other words to me. I laid in silence, hoping to hear His voice again.

Have you ever wondered why God ask you to do certain things, in precise ways? If you are like me, you may wonder, but you do not ask God, why. You just do it. I believe the correlation between the Lord's Prayer and Psalm 23 is that prayer is preamble in all things. Prayer is communicating with God. It is asking that our *will* align with the *will* of God. Prayer is connecting with our Father, who is the first and the last; the beginning and the ending. Prayer is our secret weapon. Prayer is the door that allows us to enter into the presence of our Lord. "Behold, I am the Lord, the God of all flesh: is there anything too hard for me?" (Jeremiah 32:27).

The Lord's Prayer is a model prayer that teaches us how to pray. According to Ephesians 6:18, "Praying always with all prayer and supplication in the Spirit, and watching thereunto with all perseverance and supplication for all saints." We know not what to ask God for, but the

Spirit makes intercessions for us. Therefore, the *spirit* is the vehicle that connects us to God through prayer, thereby building a spiritual relationship that blesses our understanding with the wisdom that the *Lord* [the Highest] is our shepherd and our strength.

In the Lord's Prayer, we ask God to deliver us from evil. In Psalm 23, the shepherd watches over His sheep, so that we are not led astray by evil. When turmoil comes, we seek God in prayer. We shall walk through the valley of the shadow of death, and fear no evil because the shepherd will never forsake us. God the Father, 'I AM.'

After reflecting on the prayer, I focused on the writing assignment from God. I found in the Bible everything exactly where God said it would be—not that I had any doubt in Him. Although, I had no clue how to organize the message. Nevertheless, I clicked away on my laptop. I wrote for nearly two weeks, mostly in the evenings and on weekends. After writing the initial pages of the book, I experienced writer's block. Dust began to settle on my laptop. I remember asking God for His guidance while I pondered on how to organize the message myself. I waited for a reply from God. He does not operate on our time. I concluded that God was telling me to lean on Him and He would inspire and organize His message. God will never ask us to do something and not have a plan for us to be successful in completing the task.

It took me nearly four years to write "The Great I AM." There were many obstacles from the devil that tried to prevent this message from coming to fruition. I had a few injuries that forced me to keep still, and listen to God. Praise Him! During this inspirational journey, I grew closer to Christ in spirit. There were times of pure jubilation and tears while experiencing how amazing Jesus Christ is and the power of the Word.

"The Great I AM" is written in two parts. First, the message identifies God, Jesus Christ, and the Holy Spirit as one, and as the 'I AM.' My desire is that you understand that Jesus will change your life if you allow Him to be your Savior. You will understand that you are an heir to God's throne.

You will know that Christ is working on your behalf. He is working behind the scenes, and preparing the way for you. God has the power to change your mundane life into a spirit filled life. And, Jesus is forever present and waiting for you to call upon Him.

In part 2 of "The Great I AM," the message is presented from a personal point of view based on understanding two words: *I* and *am*. Words have power. These small words can shift your life into another dimension. When you say *I am*, you are receiving the Lord's blessings, and you are speaking authority over your life. Furthermore, you are declaring and releasing your faith to believe that the Lord is empowering, inspiring, guiding, protecting, providing, and pushing you toward the destiny He has set for you.

Remember that Jesus died on an old rugged cross for our sins. He is God, who knew no sin. Your journey with Him will be a life changing experience that is spiritual rewarding each day you allow Him to be your Father. My hope is that you know our glorious Lord, and know your purpose in life. Jesus is calling. Seek the Lord in prayer and you will never want for anything. I pray that you receive revelation and spiritual transformation as you read "The Great I AM."

"For I am the Lord, your God, who takes hold of your right hand and says to you, do not fear; I will help you" (Isaiah 41:13 KJV).

"But thou, when thou prayest, enter into thy closet, and when thou hast shut thy door, pray to thy Father which is in secret; and thy Father, which seeth in secret shall reward thee openly" (Matthew 6:6).

The Lord's Prayer

Our Father, which art in Heaven, Hallowed be thy name.
Thy kingdom come.
Thy will be done in earth, as it is in Heaven.
Give us this day our daily bread,
And forgive us our debts, as we forgive our debtors.
And lead us not into temptation, but deliver us from evil: For thine is the kingdom,
and the power, and the glory, forever and ever, Amen.

Matthew 6:9-13

"My Father, which gave them me, is greater than all; and no man is able to pluck them out of my Father's hand. I and my Father are one" (John 10: 29-30).

"But whom say ye that I am?" (Matthew 16:15).

part 1

I AM the Lord's Prayer

PRAYER is the essence of your soul. Prayer helps us to recognize that we serve a higher power; someone so much larger than us. Jesus Christ, the King of kings, the Lord of lords, the Messiah, the co-designer of earth and the heavens, kneeled to his Father in prayer at the Garden of Gethsemane. His humble Spirit exemplifies the importance of prayer. Prayer is a petition to God when you communicate from the heart. Furthermore, the Lord's Prayer is the perfect prayer that teaches you how to pray because you do not know what always to say when you pray, the Spirit makes intercessions for you. You are in a spiritual battle that only Jesus can conquer.

Prayer is communion with God. Prayer teaches you to desire God's kingdom to come and His will to be done on earth as it is in heaven. When you pray, ask God to align your will according to His will as He gives you bread each day. Ask for the forgiveness of debts and forgiveness of sin as you forgive those who sin against you. Pray that you do not fall into temptation and be led to things in the world that will pull you away from Jesus. And if you succumb to sin, confess your faults, and ask for deliverance from evil. In Psalm 91:10, the scripture states, "There shall no evil befall thee, neither shall any plague come nigh thy dwelling." God is your refuge. He gives His angels charge over you for constant protection. "If thou shalt confess with thy mouth the Lord Jesus, and shalt believe in thine heart that God hath raised him from the dead, thou shalt be saved" (Romans 10:9). Jesus is salvation, glory, and majesty for ever and ever. Amen.

Men ought always pray, and not faint. Luke 18:1
"And all things, whatsoever ye shall ask in prayer, believing, ye shall receive"
(Matthew 21:22).

I AM an Absolute God

GOD'S name is I AM, Yahweh, Abba, Jehovah, Lord, Father, Rabbi, the Rock, Master, Savior, Redeemer, and Jesus Christ, the Son of God. Also, I AM the good shepherd. I AM salvation. I AM God, who existed before the creation of time. He was before anything and anyone. He is "the Great I AM" who will always be absolute in power. He is the beginning and the ending. God depends on no man. He is the perfect one who is the truth, beauty, holiness, divinity, and Glory. I AM the air you breathe. I AM your hope, protection, and comfort.

I AM the perfect peace in you. I AM happiness and love. I AM amazing grace. I AM the seed planted in good soil. I AM the keys to the kingdom. I AM infinite wisdom. I AM new wine. I AM the Potter. I AM the true vine. I AM the resurrection and eternal life. I AM a lamb without blemish. I AM yesterday, today, and tomorrow. I AM the living water; if you drink, you will never thirst again. I AM "the Great I AM."

Moses said unto God, "Behold when I come unto the children of Israel, and shall say unto them, The God of your fathers hath sent me unto you; and they shall say to me, what is his name? What shall I say unto them? And God said unto Moses; I AM THAT I AM"
(Exodus 3:13-14).

"I, even I, am the Lord: and beside me, there is no savior"
(Isaiah 43:11).

I AM the Creator

I AM the architect and chief creator. The earth was without shape, empty and void of life. The spirit drifted over the waters. I AM divided light from darkness, and it was good. I AM placed a firmament in the middle of the waters to divide it. I AM called the firmament Heaven. I AM set waters under the Heaven and spoke dry land to appear in which He called Earth. The earth yielded grass, seeds, and fruit trees after its kind. I AM made seasons, days, and years. God created two great lights: the moon and the sun. I AM brought forth birds of the air, fish in the seas, and all kinds of living creatures. And it was good. Then I AM created man in His image and Eve the first woman created out of the man. God said unto them, "Be fruitful, and multiply, and replenish the earth" (Genesis 1:28). Everything 'I AM' created was good and abundant in beauty from the peak of Mount Everest--the tallest mountain in the world to the bottom of the Mariana Trench--deepest point in the Pacific Ocean. I AM is the light that burns brightly in your heart as His Spirit guides you in harmony. Glory to I AM, the Creator.

And he arose, and rebuked the wind, and said unto the sea, "Peace, be still." And the wind ceased, and there was a great calm (Mark 4:39).

"Fear thou not; for I am with thee: be not dismayed; for I am thy God. I will strengthen thee; yea, I will help thee; yea, I will uphold thee with the right hand of my righteousness" (Isaiah 41:10).

Out of Zion, the perfection of beauty, God hath shined. Psalm 50:2

I AM the Covenant of Redemption

THE word *Trinity* is used here to identify God the Father, Jesus Christ the Son, and the Holy Spirit is one vehicle, yet having different relationships with you. Trinity is Latin meaning three in one unit. God, Father, Jesus Christ, and the Holy Spirit shares a co-equal spiritual agreement. A covenant is an agreement between two or more people. God created man in His image, but man is not equal to God, and God does not owe any obligation to humanity. God established a covenant of redemption with Jesus and the Holy Spirit. God placed a clause in the contract that promised Jesus would defeat the devil, conquer death, and return to His rightful position in heaven with all power. Lastly, the Holy Spirit seals the covenant of salvation between Jesus Christ and humanity. Christ died for your sins. In Ephesians 1:13, "In whom ye also trusted, after that, ye heard the word of truth, the gospel of your salvation: in whom also after [that] ye believed, ye were sealed with [that] holy Spirit of promise."

You live in the *New Testament,* which is the new *will* Christ left for you. Jesus says, "If a man loves me, he will keep my words: and my Father will love him. We will come unto him, and make our abode with him" (John 14:23). Your belief in Christ is essential, through obedience and faith. You are now under the covenant of *grace.* God gives you eternal blessings and eternal love. And all those that come to Christ shall remain faithful. Jesus underwent temptation from the devil; then who are you? You also will suffer temptation. In Hebrews 3:14, "For we are made partakers of Christ, if we hold the beginning of our confidence stedfast unto the end."

"And I will establish my covenant between me and thee and thy seed after thee in their generations for an everlasting covenant, to be a God unto thee, and to thy seed after thee" (Genesis 17:7).

I AM Jesus, the Christ

UNDERSTANDING Jesus Christ will be revealed to you as you study the Word and learn that He is the Word of God. In Proverbs 20:15, "There is gold, and a multitude of rubies: but the lips of knowledge are a precious jewel." By His great love, you have salvation. Your work does not warrant salvation that comes only from the Lord. You have nothing to boast about over anyone else. What God can do for you, He can do for others. Your trust in Christ builds a relationship with Him. You have the blessed assurance and the peace of knowing that the presence of God is with you. Whether you are in the core of the earth, or on the farthest planet in the universe, just whisper the name Jesus, and He is there.

The invitation to receive salvation is for everyone who believes Jesus died for you. You will hunger for the word of God in your desire to know Him better. The more you study and obey God's word, the more you will put on the traits of Christ. Jesus becomes bigger in your life as you witness to others that He is Lord. The scripture states in Matthew 11:29, "Take my yoke upon you, and learn of me; for I am meek and lowly in heart: and ye shall find rest unto your souls." In Jesus, you have the confidence of knowing you serve a living God. "That at the name of Jesus every knee should bow, of things in heaven, and things in earth, and things under the earth" (Philippians 2:10). No one will be able to escape the Lord; no one will have the opportunity to say I never had a chance to receive salvation.

In whom we have boldness and access with confidence by the faith of him.
Ephesians 3:12

"And that every tongue should confess that Jesus Christ is Lord, to the glory of God the Father" (Philippians 2:11).

I AM a Great Redeemer

JESUS, you are Lord, Savior, and the Redeemer of those who believe. Still many doubt you are the Messiah. If you are a doubter, stop reading and call on the name of Jesus. In John 8:36, the scripture says, "If the Son, therefore, shall make you free, ye shall be free indeed." If you continue in Jesus, you will be His disciple indeed. You must push to finish the race ahead of you. Be strong when times get tough and friends turn away; when people tell you that you are crazy because all your talk is about Jesus; and when people say you are paranoid for putting your trust in God, who you cannot see. It is okay, do not stop believing in the Lord.

Keep holding on because Jesus is creating new opportunities in your life. He is giving you new ideas. He is opening doors for you to meet new people who will help you veer toward the destiny He has prepared for you. You do not have to wonder how things will work out or how you will receive the resources you need to proceed. If God gives you an idea, He will also give you the tools to succeed. If God places you in a position that you know you are not qualified to have, do not worry, He will provide the talent and skills you need to be successful. He is your source, your God, and great redeemer.

Christ hath redeemed us from the curse of the law, being made a curse for us: for it is written, Cursed is every one that hangeth on a tree. Galatians 3:13

"That if thou shalt confess with thy mouth the Lord Jesus, and shalt believe in thine heart that God raised him from the dead, thou shalt be saved" (Romans 10:9).

I AM a Miracle Working God

THE Israelites turned a forty-day journey in the wilderness, into a forty year journey because of their unbelief and disobedience. The Israelites may have meandered in the desert for forty years, but not one Israelite faced sickness. God sent a disease, killing thousands of Israelites because of their disobedience and greed. The presence of God was a pillar of cloud by day, and a pillar of fire by night for warmth and guidance. God's hand was upon them with mercy and grace. The Lord blessed them with protection, meat, water, health, counseling, strength, and the Sabbath. The Israelites' clothes nor their shoes tattered during the journey. Nevertheless, the Israelites refused to believe that God had their best interest at heart, was performing miracles on their behalf, and that He would lead them to the Promised Land.

God is still in the miracle business. He is performing miracles and blessings, and it is never enough for some people, the same as with the Israelites; hard-hearted. Many refuse to say that Jesus Christ is the Savior. You have mercy and grace. It is a blessing to have the strength to get out of bed, have good health and have food to eat. Continue to walk in faith, fear God, be thankful, be obedient, and love one another. Jesus is dispatching armies of angels to take care of you. The Lord has put everything under your feet. You have the authority to command the power of the Word to work in your life. You are a miracle. El-Olam—the Everlasting God.

"Rabbi, we know that thou art a teacher come from God: for no man can do these miracles that thou doest, except God be with him" (John 3:2).

"The Lord shall fight for you" (Exodus 14:14).

I AM Everlasting Love

THE intent of making man was to seal an eternal spiritual relationship with God, Jesus, and the Spirit. God said, "Let *us* make man in *our* image, after *our* likeness" (Genesis 1:26). Following the creation of man, God removed a rib from Adam and created Eve, a wife for Adam. Suspended in the midst of the Garden of Eden was a tree that produced delicious fruit—the tree of knowledge of good and evil. God told Adam that the day he eat from this tree, he will surely die. The serpent was the most cunning of all the creatures in the garden. The serpent said to Eve, "Ye shall not surely die" (Genesis 3:4). Eve ate from the tree and encouraged Adam to eat the fruit. Immediately after eating the forbidden fruit, they died a spiritual death.

To rectify the shift in the relationship between Adam and God, Jesus Christ the Son of God became the sacrificial lamb in the *New Testament* to set things back in order as intended in the *Old Testament*. The first Adam in the Garden of Eden brought spiritual death to humanity; the second Adam, Jesus Christ brought spiritual life back to humanity. The scripture says, "I and my Father are one" (John 10:30). In John 1:15, John the Baptist declares, "This was He of whom I spake, He that cometh after me is preferred before me: for he was before me." Christ's crucifixion was for the sins of man, and to rekindle the eternal relationship with God.

"Let us make man in our image, after our likeness: and let them have dominion over the fish of the sea, and over the fowl of the air, and over the cattle, and over all the earth, and over every creeping thing that creeps upon the earth" (Genesis 1:26).

Then said Jesus, "Father, forgive them, for they know not what they do" (Luke 23:34).

I AM Milk and Honey

YOUR latter days will be greater than your former days. The Lord is with you when you face difficult challenges. The Lord is present when you feel hopeless, and your friends abandon you, and when you are trying to fight off attacks from the devil. God is there when you go through tribulation without complaining. The Lord ask that you continue to trust Him deep within your heart. He will bring you out of your troubles. He will not only bring you out, but He will bring you out better than you were before. He will lead you into a land flowing with milk and golden honey. You will move from a time of not having enough, to a time of having more than enough, and you will understand that it comes only from Christ, I AM.

Jesus is El Shaddai, the great one who is sufficient for the needs of man. You will live a better life when you worship Jesus in spirit and truth. He will give you abundance where all is lacking. He will lead you into green pastures. He will bless you going out and coming in. According to Revelation 21:4, "God shall wipe away all tears from their eyes. There shall be no more death, neither sorrow, nor crying, neither shall there be any more pain: for the former things are passed away." You are rich in faith and an heir to the kingdom of God.

How sweet are thy words unto my taste! Yea, sweeter than honey to my mouth!
Psalm 119:103

If the LORD delight in us, then he will bring us into this land, and give it us; a land that flows with milk and honey. Numbers 14:8

"He that believeth on me, as the scripture hath said, out of his belly shall flow rivers of living water" (John 7:38).

I AM the Bread of Life

THE bread you eat fills your stomach when you are hungry. As an heir of God, you know the bread of life is Jesus Christ. He is the living Word that gives you spiritual strength. It is the Word that fills you and keeps you on the straight and narrow road to eternal life. The bread you eat and the water you drink is required to preserve life for several days, but this is temporary, and eventually death results from starvation if you do not keep eating and drinking. The Lord says, "I am the bread of life; he that cometh to me shall never hunger; and he that believeth on me shall never thirst" (John 6:35).

Jesus is the spiritual bread and now sits at the right hand of God in Heaven. He gave His life so that you might have life. You cannot have a life after death without having a relationship with Jesus Christ. It is essential to hear and read God's Word every day. Natural bread eventually decays, but Jesus Christ, who is the spiritual bread of life, is eternal. Jesus knew no sin, yet became sin so that you may become righteous. The blood of Jesus cleanseth you of sins and transgressions. God forbid if any man continues to walk in sin; for sin is insubordination against God. The word of God asks you not to sin, but if anyone sins, you have an advocate, Jesus Christ the righteous.

For what the law could not do, in that it was weak through the flesh, God sending his own Son in the likeness of sinful flesh, and for sin, condemned sin in the flesh: that the righteousness of the law might be filled in us, who walk not after the flesh but after the Spirit. Romans 8:3-4

And Jesus said unto them, "I am the bread of life: he that cometh to me shall never hunger; and he that believeth on me shall never thirst" (John 6:35).

I AM the Good Shepherd

JESUS Christ is the *Good Shepherd*, who guides you through life's highs and lows. When you sense defeat, I AM is the voice cheering, "You can do it." He keeps you focused on the task. The Lord is a bit like your father on earth. When you are asked to do something, your dad expects obedience. If you do not move, there will be consequences. God is the same way. He is a good Father, who wants you to obey Him, so better things come to you. He wants you to do the right thing. He wants you to enjoy doing right. In a time of distress, it may look as if you are alone, but you are not. The devil plays on your emotions. He uses your faults to try and defeat you. God is here to fight your battles. He is your strength. Remember this: the Lord will never leave your side. In Matthew 18:11, "For the Son of man is come to save that which was lost."

The devil is not your friend, and he will never be your friend. Do not act like you are afraid of the devil. God's angels are surrounding you. The Shepherd knows when you are in trouble. In Matthew 18:12, "If a man have a hundred sheep, and one of them be gone astray, doth he not leave the ninety-nine, and goeth into the mountains, and seeketh that which is gone astray?" The Lord finds that one lost sheep and Heaven rejoices. Listen to the voice of the Lord; He is asking you to follow Him to green pastures. If you stray, He will bring you back into the sheepfold. God gave His life for your life; He will not let you face evil alone.

"I am the good shepherd: the good shepherd giveth his life for the sheep. But he that is an hireling, and not the shepherd, whose own the sheep are not, seeth the wolf coming, and leaveth the sheep, and fleeth: and the wolf catcheth them and scattereth the sheep. The hireling fleeth, because he is an hireling, and careth not for the sheep" (John 10:11-13).

I AM the Door

ON the television show, Let's Make a Deal, the announcer calls a couple from the audience to negotiate a deal with the show's host. After the first deal, if it is significant in value, the contestants may opt to choose a door on stage to win a prize of greater value. In the spiritual realm, Jesus is the door; the priceless gift is salvation, and heaven is the big stage. When you accept Jesus as the door to life, you will never lose. Jesus says in John 10:9, "I am the door; by me, if any man enters in, he shall be saved, and shall go in and out, and find pasture."

Jesus is calling you to come through the door—one way and one door that leads to heaven. Jesus is asking you to come and receive great joy, eternal hope, love, lifelong protection, healing, and the power to fight off demons. He is an ever present God waiting to lead you to higher ground. If anyone desires to remain in sin and tries to enter Heaven any other way except through the door God has created, they are the same as robbers and thieves. Jesus says in Isaiah 55:6, "Seek ye the LORD while he may be found, call ye upon him while he is near." Whisper the name of Jesus and He hears your voice. The throne room of heaven awaits you.

Jesus said, "Verily, verily, I say unto you, I am the door of the sheep. All that ever came before me are thieves and robbers: but the sheep did not hear them. I am the door: by me, if any man enters in, he shall be saved, and shall go in and out, and find pasture" (John 10:7-9).

Thus said the LORD, "Stand ye in the ways, and see, and ask for the old paths, where is the good way, and walk therein, and ye shall find rest for your souls" (Jeremiah 6:16).

I AM the Light

WHEN you enter a dark room, you cannot see what is in the room. Although your eyes are an amazing organ; the pupil adjusts to sudden light or darkness. When very dim light stimulates your eyes, the pupil opens wider, emitting more light into the eye. Without Christ, who is light, we walk in danger. Jesus helps you see darkness [evil] in the world. He opens your eyes wider; light will always conquer darkness. You can distinguish wrong from right and good from evil. Jesus gives you a new attitude, and you walk with confidence, knowing that you are not walking alone. I AM walks beside you and in you.

Jesus is the light that gives you sight. His Word is the light that opens your eyes to see the devil is a big lie. The devil is evil and represents everything that is opposite of Jesus. When you follow Christ, you will never walk in darkness; if you stumble, He will be there to catch you. A saint is just a sinner who falls but gets back up again. Jesus is the Lamb, who puts His children back on the road to righteousness. To love anything more than Him is death. The devil will try every way possible, to persuade you to love the world rather than love Jesus Christ. Fear not, Jesus is at the helm navigating your safe passage to heaven. He is a great captain.

"If any man walks in the day, he stumbleth not, because he seeth the light of the world" (John 11:9).

Then this is the message which we have heard of him, and declares unto you, that God is light, and in him is no darkness at all. 1 John 1:5

I AM a Solid Foundation

A house deteriorates when the foundation crumbles. A house declines when the roof leaks, plumbing leaks, air conditioner leaks, the foundation cracks, and drywall cracks. If the owner does not repair the house, mold and mildew will accumulate on the walls and ceiling causing health hazards to the occupants. When the foundation is infested with bugs and weeds, the house becomes dilapidated and unlivable.

The body is similar to a house that declines in health when forgotten. The body requires a nutritious diet, sunlight, exercise, water, and an annual visit to the doctor. Although the body may be in excellent health, your spirit does not have an express ticket to heaven. The spiritual person must be fed. The body deteriorates when the Lord is absent. Jesus Christ is the solid rock. The devil comes only to kill and destroy. When you believe in your heart that Jesus is your Savior, the Holy Spirit enters the soul and cleans up the house. Demons scatter to find a new home. The Holy Spirit takes away the desire for drugs, lying, stealing, cheating, and infidelity. The Holy Spirit clears away spider webs, dirt, mildew, and clutter. Behold, old things pass away, and all things become new. You are no longer living your old life, but you are now living a new life. Jesus is the only one that can lay a solid foundation. You are certified and sealed by Jesus Christ, the rock.

"And everyone that hears these sayings of mine, and doeth them not, shall be likened unto a foolish man, which built his house upon the sand" (Matthew 7:26).

For we are laborers together with God; ye are God's husbandry, ye are God's building. 1 Corinthians 3:9

I AM Calling You

JESUS desires you to make Him your first love. He is calling you to come as you are and rely totally on Him to orchestrate your life. I suggest you yield to His call. While it is said, "Today if ye will hear his voice, harden not your hearts, as in the provocation" (Hebrews 3:15). The world will know you are His disciple by your love. In James 2:18, "Yea, a man may say, Thou hast faith, and I have works: shew me thy faith without thy works, and I will shew thee my faith by my works." Do not try to promote yourself and leave the Lord out. Jesus is your source. In John 10:25, Jesus answered them, "I told you, and ye believed not: the works that I do in my Father's name, they bear witness of me."

You will know your inherent abilities and utilize the gifts Christ placed in you. Your calling is what you yearn for the most. What is your calling? Is it something that involves giving back to others? Your passion might be to visit the sick, preach or teach God's Word. Jesus wants you to see things from a spiritual perspective. Expand your vision; learn to walk by faith and not by what you see. Start looking harder at the things you cannot see. The Holy Spirit will guide you. Learn to talk to Jesus and expect God to respond. Share your deepest thoughts and fears (although He knows them already). You are on your way to higher heights and deeper depths in God. Do not worry; you will know the purpose of your calling that leads to your destiny.

And I have filled him with the spirit of God, in wisdom, and in understanding, and in knowledge, and in all manner of workmanship. Exodus 31:3

I AM the Spirit of Wisdom

GOD is the Spirit of wisdom. He is the discerner. He is the ultimate ruler who guides you in all decision-making. Study God's word diligently and allow the scriptures to saturate your mind, your heart, and your soul to help you understand your purpose. When you know, it is not about you, but it is about Jesus when you see where He is taking you, your soul will cry out in joy. When you connect in spirit with Jesus, you will decrease and Jesus increase. When you know who you are in Christ, you will know the power of I AM is leading you.

God will never ask you to do something and leave you to figure it out alone. He has a plan for success. He wants you to lead and not follow, and to be the head and not the tail. He intends to bless every part of your life: whether it is your career, your business, your marriage, your family, or your finances. God is arranging things that will help you accomplish the dreams He placed in your heart. He is absent in the flesh but with you in spirit. Trust Jesus to be with you every step of the way. He will bless you with the wisdom you need to succeed.

That the God of our Lord Jesus Christ, the Father of glory, may give unto you the spirit of wisdom and revelation in the knowledge of him. Ephesians 1:17

If any of you lack wisdom, let him ask of God, that giveth to all men liberally and upbraideth not; and it shall be given him. James 1:5

I AM the Resurrection

THE Lord is "the Great I AM" and the *Resurrection*. Be thankful that His mercy allows you to rise each morning. His grace covers you like a blanket of freshly fallen snow. Be cognizant of the Lord throughout the day. Be grateful and forgiving in spirit. Rejoice and give God the praise He rightfully deserves. Ask Jesus to help you in simple as well as complex tasks. Trust Jesus and do not worry about how things will turn out because He is in control. Keep believing in Jesus even if you do not obtain the results for which you hope. Nothing happens that is a surprise to Christ. Also, nothing happens unless Jesus allows it to happen, even when He does not cause it to happen.

It sounds strange, but be thankful for the adversities in your life. Difficulties make you stronger and make you dependent on Jesus. Christ never promised you each day would smell like roses. Roses are beautiful for the first few days then they eventually wilt, and the petals fall off. In life, you will have periods of joy, and then hard times will bring bad weather: rain, gray clouds, high winds, and lightning. You begin to slump while trying to climb the mountain towering before you. When you trust Jesus, you are letting go of your problem. You are nearing the summit. Jesus can resurrect you from the storms of life.

O Lord of hosts, blessed is the man that trusteth in thee. Psalm 84:12

Jesus said unto her, "I am the resurrection, and the life: he that believeth in me, though he were dead, yet shall he live: And whosoever liveth and believes in me shall never die. Believest thou this?" (John 11:25-26).

I AM Relief

ANXIETY is an unnecessary weight that keeps you tied up in knots. Anxiety embodies stress, uneasiness, fear, worry, tension, and impatience. You encounter one problem after another and believe that there is no way out. You may give in as some do, and accept the delusion of defeat and bad luck. Then you hear that dull nagging voice saying over and over, "I cannot win for losing." All your talk turns negative, just what the devil orders. In Jesus, you are a winner and never a loser. His word is uplifting and positive.

Stress brings fear and fear is not of God. Fear is the opposite of faith. The devil wants to drive you into a state of depression. He uses fear as a mechanism of control; fear keeps your mind fixated on the problem. God tells you to take no thought about what you will eat, drink, or wear. Jesus knows what you need and when you need it. Seek first the kingdom of God. Do not worry about tomorrow; tomorrow will take care of itself. In fact, you will learn how to live free of anxiety. Let "the Great I AM" be the relief you are searching for; He will lighten your load—if you trust Him. Christ's Holy Word gives you comfort, assurance, harmony, inspiration, and vision. Antacid Medicine provides temporary relief of acid indigestion. "The Great I AM" offers permanent relief from stress related symptoms.

"Therefore, take no thought, saying, What shall we eat? Or, What shall we drink? Or Wherewithal shall we be clothed? (For after these things do the Gentiles seek) for your Heavenly Father knows that ye have need of all these things. But seek ye first the kingdom of God, and his righteousness; and all these things shall be added unto you. Take therefore no thought for the morrow: for the morrow shall take thought for the things of itself. Sufficient unto the day is the evil thereof" (Matthew 6:31-34).

I AM a Friend Always

IN the world, a friend is someone you care about and enjoy being around. A friend is someone who hears you and is there for you in troubled times. A friend is someone who tells you what is right when you may not want to listen. A friend is someone who is trustworthy. Take a few moments and think about your childhood friends in elementary school; now think about the friends you have now. This person may be a spouse or someone else you know. Does this person have the characteristics of a friend? If so, this person is your BF: best friend. Unlike friends in the world who might come and go--a friend today and an enemy tomorrow. Jesus was your friend before you were born. He is your eternal best friend now and forever.

Jesus is a lamp unto your feet that guides you through seen and unseen dangers. He will never break His trust. When Jesus conquered death, He took back the keys: authority and power. Christ's mission was complete. Jesus gave you the keys. He is the way to eternal life. He is the mark of the high calling which is virtuous, pure, and holy. The Lord is a friend who is present with you always. "Greater love hath no man than this; that a man lay down his life for his friends" (John 15:13).

O give thanks unto the LORD; for he is good: because his mercy endureth forever.
Psalm 118:1

Jesus said unto him; "I am the way, the truth, and the life: no man cometh unto the Father, but by me" (John 14:6).

"As long as I am in the world, I am the light of the world" (John 9:5).

I AM the Keys to the Kingdom

A lock is designed to ensure only the owner or occupant has access to their property. Some buildings require different locks for each door. The occupant has possession of a key that only unlocks his or her door. The owner of the building has a master key that opens every lock on the grounds. Jesus holds the master key that opens the locked door to the kingdom. In God's house, there are many mansions. Jesus possesses the key to every door in His mansions. And if any person desires to live in Christ's mansion, you must be born again. And, you must accept Jesus as the Savior and His sacrifice made for you.

As an heir of Christ, you have the authority and power to speak the word of God, and it is activated immediately carrying out your request according to the Bible. As an heir, you have privileges here on earth. Matthew 7:7, states, "Ask, and it will be given to you; seek and you will find; knock and it will be open to you." You have the scriptures in the Bible, deliverance, prosperity, and protection from a host of angels ready to triumph over evil for you. Jesus gives you authority and the prayer of faith. "Verily I say unto you, Whatsoever ye shall bind on earth shall be bound in heaven: and whatsoever ye shall loose on earth shall be loosed in heaven" (Matthew 18:18). The acceptance of Jesus Christ says you have the authorization to call upon God's promises. When two or more agree in Jesus' name, He is with you. Praise God.

Again I say unto you, "That if two of you shall agree on earth as touching anything that they shall ask, it shall be done for them of my Father which is in heaven. For where two or three are gathered together in my name, there am I in the midst of them" (Matthew 18:19-20).

I AM the True Vine

B OTANY is the study of plant life. Typically, a seed is planted in soil, fertilized, and watered to develop. Also, plants need sunlight to become a healthy tree. In time, the tree grows branches, vines, leaves, and produce fruits or nuts. The vine must be sturdy enough to bear weight. In the Old Testament, God was the first botanist who created the Garden of Eden. His garden probably produced every kind of plant and tree imaginable. In the New Testament, Jesus is the true vine, and you are the branches. Unlike fruit growth from seeds that usually produce differently from its parent fruit. As a seed of Christ, you are an exact likeness of Him; you must abide in Jesus. A fruit tree that does not bear fruit is cut down and destroyed. Jesus provides food for the birds and fowl of the air. He is more than able to provide for you no matter what misfortunes you might encounter.

Christ's disciples were the fruit of the vine chosen to spread the gospel. In Matthew 10:14, Jesus told his disciples, "And whosoever shall not receive you, nor hear your words, when ye depart out of that house or city, shake off the dust of your feet." Now, you are the fruit of the vine connected to Jesus. Your purpose is to help spread the gospel. You cannot do anything without Christ. And the Lord said, "If you had faith as a grain of mustard seed, ye might say unto this sycamine tree, Be plucked up by the root, and be thou planted in the sea, and it should obey you" (Luke 17:6). The mustard seed is the tiniest seed that grows to become large in stature. Your faith starts as a flickering flame, yet it can grow stronger and brighter in Christ as you continue in His love.

"Herein is my Father glorified that ye bear much fruit; so shall ye be my disciples. As the Father hath loved me, so have I loved you: continue ye in my love" (John 15:8-9).

I AM Alpha and Omega

GOD is the Alpha and Omega, the beginning and the end of everything that exists. God created the Heavens and earth. He created every living organism from the tiniest cell to the largest sea life. He created man out of the dust of the earth. Adam was lifeless until God breathed the breath of life into his nostrils. You were dead in sin. God breathed His breath [life] in you. "And this is life eternal, that they might know thee, the only true God, and Jesus Christ, whom thou hast sent" (John 17:3).

God created everything that the eyes can see, and the hand can touch. As a believer, you know that life is not possible without God. The incredibly wealthy go to great measures to avoid aging and dying. The gift of eternal life comes from God. The devil comes only to take and destroy. The scripture in John 10:10 says, "I am come that they might have life and that they might have it more abundantly." Behold, the wicked shall see the second coming of Jesus Christ who is the atonement of sin. The ungodly will see Him as the mighty I AM. God did not give you a spirit of fear, but a spirit of power and might. Fear not; God is with you always.

Behold, he cometh with clouds; and every eye shall see him, and they also which pierced him: and all kindred of the earth shall wail because of him. Even so, Amen. "I am Alpha and Omega, the beginning, and the ending, that is, and which was, and which is to come, the Almighty" (Revelation 1:7-8).

"Fear not; I am the first and the last. I am he that lives and was dead; and, behold, I am alive for evermore, Amen: and have the keys of hell and death" (Revelation 1:17-18).

I AM the Bright and Morning Star

GOD is the bright and morning star. Light comes to everyone who believes Jesus as Lord and Savior. The Lord is the light of the world to those who choose to walk in His marvelous light and enjoy the peace of His presence. In I Am, there is not a hint of darkness—as opposed to the devil who is the ruler of darkness in this world. The brightness of Christ illuminates the sinful deeds hidden in the heart of man.

According to 2 Timothy 1:10, "Our Savior Jesus Christ, who hath abolished death, and hath brought life and immortality to light through the gospel." Immortal life is a gift to everyone sanctified in Christ. Do not fear death. Fear is the opposite of faith. "So then faith cometh by hearing, and hearing by the word of God" (Romans 10:17). Whom shall you fear? The Word of the Lord is manifest throughout the world. According to Philippians 2:11, "Every tongue should confess that Jesus Christ is Lord, to the glory of God the Father." God's sheep knows the voice of God. "Resist the devil and he will flee from you" (James 4:7).

"I am the root and the offspring of David, and the bright and morning star"
(Revelation 22:16).

"The Lord is my light and my salvation; whom shall I fear? The Lord is the strength of my life; of whom shall I be afraid?" (Psalm 27:1).

"For God has not given us a spirit of fear; but of power, and of love, and of a sound mind" (2 Timothy 1:7).

I AM the Lord, and I Change Not

THE world changes quickly, and when you take your eyes off the Lord and choose the way of the world, you change quickly too. The spirit is willing, but the flesh is weak. An indecisive mind that changes like the wind become vulnerable to the evil things in the world. In 1 John 2:15, "Love not the world, neither the things that are in the world. If any man love the world, the love of the Father is not in him." Loving both the world, and God is impossible. You will obey one and not the other. The scripture tells you to mark the perfect man, Jesus. The Lord is the supreme ruler, and He changes not. I AM is the same yesterday, today, and always. God created the universe, and He created you with the power of His Word. "Bless the Lord, O my soul" (Psalm 104:1).

Your afflictions keep you close to the Lord. You are not able to live a blessed life without Jesus. Whether it is in your professional or personal life, you need the Lord to help you take bold steps to become more than a conqueror. How many times would you have called on Jesus if things were perfect in your life? That was not a trick question. Jesus confounds the wicked with the mundane things of this world and gives His elect wisdom. Learn to depend on Jesus in desperate situations. God makes you strong when you are most vulnerable. The Lord will never abandon you. Remember that change is constant and you will have conflicts while residing in this world. Trust in God who will never change.

"For I am the LORD, I change not" (Malachi 3:6).

"No man can serve two masters: for either he will hate the one, and love the other; or else he will hold to the one, and despise the other. Ye cannot serve God and mammon" (Matthew 6:24).

I AM Prayer S.O.S

PRAYER is an essential element in worship. Jesus prayed to God, His Father while He was on earth. The disciples asked Christ to teach them how to pray. Whether you walk with the Lord or not, you should pray. Jesus said to Peter in Matthew 26:41, "Watch and pray, that ye enter not into temptation: the spirit indeed is willing, but the flesh is weak." The Lord will put no more on you than you can bear. Call on Jesus for help. He wants you to trust Him. When you ask anything in Christ's name, if it is in the Word, He will provide. Do not disobey God. "Now unto him, that is able to do exceeding abundantly above all that we ask or think, according to the power that worketh in us" (Ephesians 3:20).

God's Word is the blueprint for help. Lord, how great thou are? "I am a great King," said the Lord of hosts in Malachi 1:14. God's Word encourages you to pray in season and out of season. Prayer is nourishment for the body and food for the soul. It is a necessity to communicate with God every day. He knows what things you need before you pray. Jesus promises to supply all your needs. It gives the Lord joy when you remind him of His promises to you. It says in 2 Timothy 2:15, "Study to show thyself approved unto God, a workman that needeth not to be ashamed, rightly dividing the word of truth." I AM desires to bless you and take you to a higher plateau closing in on your flight to heaven.

"That he would grant you, according to the riches of his glory, to be strengthened with might by his Spirit in the inner man"
(Ephesians 3:16).

I AM Your Refuge

THE Lord is my refuge. He that dwells in the secret place of the highest shall abide under the shadow of the Almighty. I will say of the LORD; He is my shelter and my stronghold: my God; I trust. Surely He shall deliver me from the trap of the fowler, and from the noisome pestilence. He shall cover me with His feathers, and under His wings will I trust: His truth will be my armor and buckler (Psalm 91:1-4).

I am in the hands of the Lord. I shall not be afraid for the terror by night; nor for the arrow that flies by day; nor for the pestilence that walks in evil; nor for the destruction that wasteth at midday. A thousand will fall at my side, and ten thousand at my right hand; but it will not come near me. Only with my eyes will I see the reward of the wicked. Because the LORD is my refuge, even the highest, my habitation. No evil shall come against me, neither shall any plague come near my dwelling. The Lord shall give his angels charge over me (Psalm 91:5-11). The "Great I AM" is my refuge always.

With long life will I satisfy him, and show him my salvation.
Psalm 91:16

The Lord is my strength and my song, and he has become my salvation. He is my God, and I will prepare him an habitation; my father's God, and I will exalt him.
Exodus 15:2

I AM Your Father in Heaven

JESUS is often sought after more in tough times than in happy times when life appears to be grand. Seek the Lord especially when times are good. In fact, you should have endless praise for Him always. Jesus is your provider. He shields you from evil. Remember, Jesus cares deeply about His children. He listens to your concerns. The Lord waits for you to bring Him your worst fears. He is Abba Father. He will carry you through difficulties. Trust Him with your heart. Keep your mind on Jesus, and remember that trouble is near.

Jesus never promised you that your life would be free of problems. He never promised you everlasting peace and joy in this world. Thank the Lord. The greater the problem, the closer He is. It is even better to praise God before misery knocks on your door. Continue to praise God when the devil tells you your praise is not working and God does not hear you. When you hear this, shout back at the devil that you do not mind waiting on the LORD. Start praising Jesus more earnestly than you ever have before. Jesus says, "Come unto me all ye that labor and are heavy laden, and I will give you rest. Take my yoke upon you, and learn of me; for I am meek and lowly in heart, and ye shall find rest unto your souls. For my yoke is easy, and my burden is light" (Matthew 11:28-30). Trust Jesus to orchestrate your steps. You serve an immense God.

The troubles of my heart are enlarged: O bring thou me out of my distresses.
Psalm 25:17

For my soul is full of troubles: and my life draws nigh unto the grave. Psalm
88:3

I AM Faithful

A CCORDING to John 10:10, "I am come that they might have life and that they might have it more abundantly." God's Word provides encouragement, stability, and strength. All things are possible with I AM. The Lord will never harm you, unlike the one who walks in darkness. The devil comes only to destroy. There is no situation in life that God did not conquer. Jesus carried every challenge to the cross that you might face. Jesus can resolve any dilemma in your life. It does not matter whether it is your family, sickness, habits, loneliness, grief, or despair. Greater is the faith of those who have not seen Christ, and yet they believe. God wants your heart woven in His love. Your belief that Jesus is the Savior shows the world that your way of doing things is over, and you are willing to allow God to guide your heart. Christ's precious grace and love overshadow your old life. Jesus will never leave you. He is your advocate and your guiding light. Who will you fear? The Lord is your strength and protection.

For ye are dead, and your life is hidden with Christ in God.
Colossians 3:3

But these are written, that ye might believe that Jesus is the Christ, the Son of God; and that believing, ye might have life through his name. John 20:31

Thy word is a lamp unto my feet, and a light unto my path.
Psalm 119:105

I AM Praise and Thanks

IF you knew everything Jesus Christ has done for you since you were created, you would not be able to give God all the praise and thanks for His plethora of blessings. You would never have enough praise for the miracles, and healings God has performed in your life. "In everything give thanks: for this is the will of God in Christ Jesus concerning you" (1 Thessalonians 5:18). Give thanks to the Lord, for He is good, and His love is everlasting. "Let Israel now say that his mercy endures forever. Let the house of Aaron now say that his mercy endures forever" (Psalm 118:2-3).

Give thanks unto Jesus because He gave His life for you. Without Him you are nothing. Give thanks to unseen blessings in your life. Let those who fear the Lord say, "To him who alone doeth great wonders: for his mercy endureth forever" (Psalm 136:4). Give thanks to Jesus for His amazing grace, His mercy, and wisdom. While in tribulation, call upon Him, and He will answer you. Trust Jesus to reveal the wonderful plans He has ready for you. When you sincerely believe Jesus, you will never be the same. When you serve Christ, who is greater than you, you will understand your identity in Him. Galatians 6:18 states, "Brethren, the grace of our Lord Jesus Christ be with your spirit. Amen."

Looking for that blessed hope, and the glorious appearing of the great God and our Savior Jesus Christ; Who gave himself for us, that he might redeem us from all iniquity, and purify unto himself a peculiar people, zealous of good works. Titus 2:13-14

Now, therefore, our God, we thank thee and praise thy glorious name. 1 Chronicles 29:13

I AM the Lamb

JOHN the Baptist, a Nazarite, who dressed in a camel's hair garment, ate locust and wild honey and was anointed with the Holy Spirit before his birth. John was a prophet and a disciple of Jesus Christ. He baptized sinners who were sorry for their sins. Baptism symbolizes washing away sin and the beginning of a new life dedicated to serving God. John, preached the coming of Jesus, who is mightier than him whose shoes he is not worthy to untie. One glorious day John saw Jesus coming toward him and shouted, "Behold the Lamb of God, which taketh away the sin of the world" (John 1:29). Jesus shall baptize with the Holy Ghost and with fire.

Jesus preached about the Kingdom of Heaven, healed the sick, opened the eyes of the blind, and performed miracles before the masses. Thousands believed Jesus was the Messiah, and yet many did not believe Christ was the Messiah, which is similar to many unbelievers today. Around the world, people will hear the gospel of Christ and still deny that Jesus is the *Lamb of God*. In John 6:36, "But I said unto you, that ye also have seen me, and believe not." Jesus is "the Great I AM" the son of God. Jesus bled for you on the cross and won the war over sin. Jesus Christ is the Savior of man. Now, it is up to you to believe that He will fight your battles.

Forasmuch as ye know that ye were not redeemed with corruptible things, as silver and gold, from your vain conversation received by tradition from your fathers; But with the precious blood of Christ, as of a lamb without blemish and without spot: who verily was foreordained before the foundation of the world, but was manifest in these last times for you, who by him do believe in God, that raised him up from the dead, and gave him glory; that your faith and hope might be in God. 1 Peter 1:18-21

I AM the Conqueror

JESUS is a mighty conquering King. As a child of God, you are more than a conqueror. You have God's Holy Spirit living in you. The Holy Spirit is the ultimate gift to those who believe in Jesus. You will go places you never dreamed of going; you will do things you never dreamed of doing, and you will meet people you never dreamed of meeting. You will conqueror things you never dreamed of conquering. You will achieve your God given dreams sooner than you think. These things will happen because of the God you serve.

You are more than a conqueror. The Lord says all things are possible with Him. God does not say *a few* things are possible; He says *all* things are possible. As a conqueror, doors will open, and doors will close. Opportunities will come your way. You will get positions you are not qualified to have--God will never give you anything that He will not help you keep. As a conqueror, you will see *favor* that is beyond your comprehension. You were destined to be a conqueror before you were born. Bless God!

"As it is written, for thy sake we are killed all the day long; we are accounted as sheep for the slaughter. Nay, in all these things we are more than conquerors through him that loved us" (Romans 8:37).

"Before I formed thee in the belly I knew thee, and before thou came forth out of the womb I sanctified thee, and I ordained thee a prophet unto the nations" (Jeremiah 1:5).

I AM a Master Planner

I AM planned the world from creation to destruction. The Lord's intellect is so vast and unique compared to the mind of the greatest scientist and physician. God designed the greatest escape ever—the spiritual reconnection between God and humanity. Jesus Christ died on the cross, was buried, and rose in three days with all power. Our Lord, Jesus Christ, who is greater than Houdini. "When he ascended up on high, he led captivity captive" (Ephesians 4:8). According to the *Old Testament*, Isaac was Abraham's promised son from God. One day, God asked Abraham to take Isaac to the top of Mt. Moriah and offer him up as a sacrifice. So, Abraham and Isaac journeyed to the top of the mountain. Isaac said to his father, "Behold the fire and the wood: but where is the lamb for a burnt offering?" Abraham replied to Isaac, "God will provide *Himself* a lamb for a burnt offering" (Genesis 22:7-8). There is a ram in the bush when situations get tight.

In the *New Testament* Jesus Christ is the Lamb of God. You are not redeemed with corruptible things such as silver and gold. "But with the precious blood of Christ, as of a lamb without blemish and spot. Who verily was foreordained before the foundation of the world, but was manifest in these last times for you" (1 Peter 1:19-20). Look up and live. Jesus is the author of your faith. Abide in Jesus Christ. "If ye love me, keep my commandments" (John 14:15). God is unconditional love, and His grace is sufficient.

Looking unto Jesus the author and finisher of our faith; who for the joy that was set before him endured the cross, despising the shame, and is set down at the right hand of the throne of God. Hebrews 12:2

I AM the Savior

I AM the Savior. It is imperative that you know Jesus loves you. Jesus desires to have a personal relationship with you. When you confess with your mouth and believe that God raised Jesus from the dead, you shall be saved. Instantly, you receive salvation. You are born of the Spirit. In John 3:3, Jesus said, "Verily, verily, I say unto thee; except a man is born again, he cannot see the kingdom of God."

All have sinned and come short of God's glory. You were far off but now made near by the blood of Jesus. Repent of your sins. You have everything to gain in Jesus and so much to lose if you do not accept Christ as your Savior. You will transform into the person the Lord knows you can be and not who others want you to be. You have the victory. Christ shows you who you are and who you can be in Him. Jesus enables you to do great things in your life and the lives of others. God is Holy, and He asks you to be holy. According to John 3:16, "Whosoever believeth in Him should not perish, but have everlasting life." Tell Jesus that you love Him.

Then said Jesus unto his disciples, "If any man will come after me, let him deny himself, and take up his cross, and follow me"
(Matthew 16:24).

Ye might believe that Jesus is the Christ, the Son of God; and that believing ye might have life through his name. John 20:31

I AM Fruit of the Spirit

DO you know the glory of I AM is the Holy Spirit living in you? Imagine that there is a present wrapped in beautiful paper and adorned with a large silk bow. The expectation builds as you anticipate what might be in the present. In time, Jesus will unwrap many facets of your life through the Holy Spirit that will thrust you forward into your destiny. Christ is the true vine, and you are the branches. Jesus is the fruit of the spirit. The Holy Spirit fills you with love, joy, peace, kindness, self-control, endurance, goodness, gentleness, and faith. You are seeds of greatness.

Jesus is endless *love*. He loves you so much that He died to set you free. He gives you eternal *joy*. Yes, you have joy in your everyday life, but in Jesus, you will have sudden laughter when you think of His goodness. You will cry when you remember the things He brought you through. Jesus fills you with *peace* the world cannot understand, especially when there is unrest. When evil is lurking, His blood covers you. Jesus also fills you with *kindness*, *goodness*, and *gentleness*. The spirit gives you *self-control*. You remain discipline when others are fighting and swearing. In 1 Corinthians 13:5, "The Spirit doth not behave itself unseemly, seeketh not her own, not easily provoked, thinketh no evil." Come humble and willing to follow the voice of Jesus Christ. Release the weights in your life and run the race with endurance.

"Howbeit when he, the Spirit of truth, is come, he will guide you into all truth: for he shall not speak of himself; but whatsoever he shall hear, that shall he speak: and he will show you things to come" (John 16:13).

I AM Power on High

THE Lord ask you to wait and receive power from on high. You serve an infinitely and wise God, who does not make mistakes. The Spirit resides deep in your soul. You will receive the power of the Holy Spirit to help you walk in faith. The Holy Spirit is always present. You have boldness, courage, confidence, and passion. The Holy Spirit enables you to do the will of God. How be it when the Spirit of truth comes? He will guide you in truth and show you things to come. How can two entities walk together unless there is harmony? The Lord tells you to turn right, and you turn left. Jesus sends you confirmation through His Word, but you still go left. You detoured from the plan. Jesus wants to put you back on track.

God is not the author of confusion. He does not play games. You must worship Him with passion and persistence. Jesus never glorified Himself, only God his Father. Be a witness to those in the world. Through the power of the Holy Spirit, not only will you do the works of I AM, but you shall do greater works. Jesus, the Son of God, fills you with power from on high. Jesus is ahead of you moving obstacles out of your way, follow I AM.

"He that believeth on me, the works that I do shall he also do; and greater works than these shall he do; because I go unto my Father"
(John 14:12).

"And, behold, I send the promise of my Father upon you: but tarry ye in the city of Jerusalem, until ye be endued with power from on high"
(Luke 24:49).

I AM the Holy Temple

YOUR body is the temple of the living God. When Jesus accepts your confession that you believe He is Christ, the Savior, a transformation begins in you. As a new Christian, you have no idea what to expect or what changes will occur in your life. Your thoughts and emotions will change as you conform to the *Will* of God. According to Philippians 2:5, "Let this mind be in you, which is also in Christ Jesus." Having the mind of Christ allows you to understand what it means to have compassion for others and the things of God. The spirit resides in the soul: the inner being of a person. You are the temple of Christ.

It is impossible to have the Spirit of God without transforming your behavior. According to Genesis 1:26, "And God said, let us make man in our image, after our likeness." You are a masterpiece. In Matthew 9:17, "Neither do men put new wine into old bottles: else the bottles will break, and the wine runneth out, and the bottles perish: but they put new wine into new bottles, and both are preserved." The Holy Spirit will not dwell in unclean places. In Roman 12:1, "I beseech you, therefore, brethren, by the mercies of God, that ye present your bodies a living sacrifice, holy, acceptable unto God, which is your reasonable service." You are a sacred vessel created in His image.

For the word of God is quick, and powerful, and sharper than any two-edged sword, piercing even to the dividing asunder of soul and spirit, and of the joints and marrow, and is a discerner of the thoughts and intents of the heart. Hebrews 4:12

"God is a Spirit, and they that worship him must worship him in spirit and in truth" (John 4:24).

I AM a Life Changer

A dramatic phenomenon occurs in the life cycle of a butterfly. In *stage one*, an adult female butterfly lays her eggs on a particular leaf. A few weeks later, *stage two* takes place when the eggs hatch into a *caterpillar*. After the caterpillar fully develops, it eats the same leaf on which it was hatched. In fact, the caterpillar eats a lot. In *stage three*, the caterpillar changes into a *chrysalis*. In *stage four*, the *chrysalis* develops into a beautiful *butterfly* or *metamorphosis*. The butterfly finds a mate, and the life cycle begins again.

A dramatic phenomenon occurs in the human life that is similar to the life cycle of the butterfly. In *stage one*, life starts with the fertilization of the female egg. In *stage two*, you are a newborn baby, then grow to become a toddler, a teenager, and a young adult. You are trying to find your identity. *Stage three* takes place as you discover that your purpose is in the Word of God. The caterpillar becomes uncomfortable as it outgrows its skin (molting). As your faith develops, you become uncomfortable in your old skin. The new butterfly tries to fly; it needs lots of practice. As a new Christian, you are learning to fly, and you need lots of practice on how to walk away from things that will hinder you. You will encounter problems you have never dealt with before as a new Christian. "And be not conformed to the world: but be ye transformed by the renewing of your mind, that ye may prove what is that good, and acceptable, and perfect, will of God" (Romans 12:2). In *stage four*, you grow to be an elderly adult. You understand what it means to worship God, and you understand servant leadership. You are preparing to pass away. You know that you are going home to be with the Lord, and eternal life begins.

"But as many as received him, to them gave he power to become the sons of God, even to them that believe on his name" (John 1:12).

I AM Reason and Season

YOUR life is purpose driven according to your destiny set by God. According to Ecclesiastes 3:2-4, "A time to be born and a time to die, a time to plant and a time to pluck up that which is planted. A time to kill, and a time to heal, a time to break down, and a time to build up. A time to weep, and a time to laugh, a time to mourn, and a time to dance." Do not get caught up in the mundane reasons of why this or that happens. God has a plan and purpose for everything. There will be some things that will overwhelm you and leave you completely befuddled. Accept God for who He is without questions or doubt. If the Word is not in you, you will become bitter toward God and blame Him for everything that goes wrong in life. Jesus will take you through each season of change with the peace of knowing you will survive. In due season, God will give you beauty for ashes. In troubled times, you must persevere.

In your darkest moment believe that Jesus knows your pain. A tractor trailer truck carries heavy cargo on highways. Truck drivers must meet state regulations by having their cargo calculated at weight stations. You will have different stages in life where God knows the weight you are carrying, and He gives you rest. Trucks carrying heavy cargo that exceed the maximum weight limit can cause road deterioration. Your body is the tractor trailer, and your heart is the vehicle's engine. An excess amount of stress can cause death. God is the scale measuring the amount of weight you are carrying. Jesus has every season of your life planned so that He can control the weight of *seen* and *unforeseen* problems. God's grace is sufficient.

To everything, there is a season and a time to every purpose under the Heaven.
Ecclesiastes 3:1

"For my yoke is easy, and my burden is light" (Matthew 11:30).

I AM One

EAT, laugh, pray, and enjoy family and friends in the time you have here on earth. Live each day unto Christ and be thankful for all things. You are in a relationship with Jesus through the shedding of His blood for your sins. You are one with I AM. Be faithful and dwell together in unity on one accord in Jesus, the Christ. It states in Psalm 95:2, "Let us come before his presence with thanksgiving, and make a joyful noise unto him with psalms." God created an earth full of splendor and beauty. The scripture says in 1 John 2:15, "Love not the world, neither the things that are in the world. If any man love the world, the love of the Father is not in him."

God's home is not of this world, and neither is yours. Jesus never lost sight of why He was in the world. He never lost sight of His Father in Heaven. You are a stranger in a foreign land marching toward Heaven. Jesus said, "Foxes have holes, and birds of the air have nests; but the Son of man hath not where to lay his head" (Luke 9:58). You should never focus solely on your house, food, clothes, or wealth. Seek to understand your purpose in life. Jesus has prepared an exclusive mansion in Heaven for your arrival. "In hope of eternal life, which God, who cannot lie, promised before the world began" (Titus 1:2). Heaven is a prepared place for prepared people.

"And now I am no more in the world, but these are in the world, and I come to thee. Holy Father, keep through thine own name those whom thou hast given me, that they may be one, as we are" (John 17:11).

I AM Hidden Treasure

A wise man makes smart investments. An Individual Retirement Account is created to secure one's financial future. God gives you common sense to make smart investments. God's Word is long-term investment and treasure filled with substance and value. In Psalm 119:11, "Thy word have I hid in mine heart, that I might not sin against thee." If you eat the Word and let the Word digest, it will bring you out of poverty and despair, and move you closer to God. It is impossible to serve God and be a failure in life. To paraphrase the senior pastor of the Potter's House and *NYT* bestselling author, T.D. Jakes: you *give up relying on instincts and begin to rely on your intellect, social experience, and logic* (Jakes, 2015). So, instead of relying on your logic, learn to rely on God—who gives you the intelligence needed to understand the hidden treasures in the Word.

You have hidden inside of you: ideas, skills, and abilities to accomplish your God-given dreams. One of the greatest treasures Christ gives is salvation. The Bible tells you not to waste time storing up treasures on earth which are prone to moths and thieves. If you trust only in worldly investments and not in God, the treasures you store will be subject to losses. As stated in Colossians 3:2, "Set your affection on things above, not on things on this earth." Trust and believe I AM who is unseen, but makes provisions for you. In John 4:24, "God is a Spirit: and they that worship him must worship him in spirit and in truth." In your heart is the riches of God's word; share this treasure with others.

"Now, therefore, if ye will obey my voice indeed, and keep my covenant, then ye shall be a peculiar treasure unto me above all people: for all the earth is mine" (Exodus 19:5).

I AM the Head of the Church

I AM is the head, and you are the body. In Ephesians 5:23, "Christ is the head of the church: and he is the savior of the body." He is the Chief Cornerstone where the church began. You are one body in Christ, just as God, his Father, and the Spirit are one. Jesus Christ, the Redeemer, who is pure and righteous. Jesus died to bestow the gift of salvation to every member whom He gives life. You are no longer called a servant of God, for the servant, knows not what his master does. Jesus calls you a friend. John 15:13 says, "Greater love hath no man than this, that a man lay down his life for his friends." Give God the glory for everything.

God will never fail you. He presented a church [Himself] void of having a spot or wrinkle. The day you are welcomed into the kingdom, you also will be holy and without blemish. Those who are sanctified will walk in His glory. Be not as the five foolish virgins who took their lamps empty of oil with them to meet the bridegroom. Be wise as the five virgins who had their lamps filled with oil. Let the anointing oil [Holy Spirit] be in your vessel to give you light out of darkness. Trim your lamp so others may know Jesus is the head of the church. It will be too late to hear the Word of God, and receive His spirit once the doors of heaven shut.

"Henceforth I call you not servants; for the servant knoweth not what his lord doeth: but I have called you friends; for all things that I have heard of my Father I have made known unto you" (John 15:15).

That he might present it to himself a glorious church, not having spot, or wrinkle, or any such thing; but that it should be holy and without blemish. Ephesians 5:27

I AM the Light of Life

G OD is the light of life. Jesus, the Son of God, is brighter than the sun He made to give light and heat on earth. God created the moon that gives light in the sky at night. He saw that the moon needed some attitude and not just altitude. He added a few billion stars to sparkle and dance around the moon. God is the light of lights. You are chosen to be a light in this world. You are crafted from the dust of the earth and placed above all things in earth. You are known to God in all His works from the beginning. Everything God made was good, except when He divided the water under the firmament from the waters which were above the firmament, He said, "It was so" (Genesis 1:7).

In 1 Peter 2:9, "But ye are a chosen generation, a royal priesthood, a holy nation, a peculiar people; that ye should shew forth the praises of him who hath called you out of darkness into his marvelous light." In Ephesians 5:8, "For ye were sometimes darkness, but now are ye light in the Lord: walk as children of light." Sin abound in those who delight in evil. God is the light of the world and in Him is no darkness. Jesus is the light of life, follow Christ and you will never walk in darkness.

Ye are all the children of light, and the children of the day: we are not of the night, nor of darkness. 1Thessalonians 5:5

"As long as I am in the world, I am the light of the world" (John 9:5).

Then spoke Jesus again unto them, saying, "I am the light of the world: he that followeth me shall not walk in darkness, but shall have the light of life" (John 8:12).

I AM a Secret Hiding Place

THE Central Intelligence Agency is a U.S. government agency focused on foreign civilian intelligence gathering. The CIA gathers, processes, analyzes, and classifies information on various individuals and entities associated with national security around the world. The president and his cabinet are privy to intelligence collected by the CIA. "The Great I AM" does not need the CIA or the FBI, or the SEC to provide Him information on what is happening in the world because He is the creator and knows all things. Jesus created the agency that created the agency. He is your Central Intelligence Agent. Jesus is the head of covert operations. He is your secret hiding place which protects you in plain sight. Jesus hides things from those who profess to be wiser than Him.

No one knows the end, but God. When Jesus rose from the grave, He announced it was finished. The Lord is your sanctuary and your stronghold. His wings of mercy and truth cover you. He has given His angels watch over you day and night. Jesus will make your enemies your footstool. He has not given you a spirit of fear, but of power and love. You have permission to *ask* anything in the name of Jesus. Remember that you wrestle not against flesh and blood but principalities, powers, and rulers of darkness, and evil in the air. The flesh is weak when you operate without Jesus. The devil steps up his plan of attack to destroy you. The devil believes he has power until God reminds him that he is nothing. The devil trembles at the name of Jesus. "Open to me the gates of righteousness: I will go into them, and I will praise the LORD" (Psalm 118:19).

For we wrestle not against flesh and blood, but against principalities, against powers, against the rulers of the darkness of this world, against spiritual wickedness in high places. Ephesians 6:12

I AM the Jet Bridge to Eternal Life

A jet bridge is an elongated movable passageway that runs from the airport terminal to the door of an airplane. Jesus is the ticket agent standing at the gate waiting to stamp your flight ticket to the third heaven. To be among the chosen few to enter heaven is a privilege. "And then shall he send his angels, and shall gather together his elect from the four winds, from the uttermost part of the earth to the uttermost part of heaven" (Mark 13:27).

You are blessed to be an inheritance of Christ. In 1 Thessalonians 4:16, "For the Lord himself shall descend from heaven with a shout, with the voice of the archangel, and with the trump of God: and the dead in Christ shall rise first." It is a blessing to be among those who will hear the great sound of the trumpet. Romans 8:33 asks, "Who shall lay anything to the charge of God's elect? It is God that justifieth." God's elect will be transported at warp speed from earth to the kingdom to live with Christ forever.

"But ye are a chosen generation, a royal priesthood, a holy nation, a peculiar people, that ye should shew forth the praises of him who hath called you out of darkness into his marvelous light. Which in time past were not a people, but are now the people of God: which had not obtained mercy, but now have obtained mercy" (1 Peter 2: 9-10).

I AM Your Repentance

IT is impossible to enter the Kingdom of God with your old ways and old thoughts intact. You must sell out to the change Jesus brings; you must adopt a mindset that desires the *will* of the Lord. The obsession for worldly things is enmity against Christ: the carnal mind is belligerent to the laws of God. However, there is no sin too great that the blood of Jesus cannot wash away. Repent while Jesus is near. Pull off the old ways and put on the characteristics of Jesus. Seek God's will and His Salvation. Desire His kingdom to come that it may fill you with righteousness, forgiveness, and the anointing Spirit of Christ.

Jesus is repentance, and you will never know the pure joy of salvation until you relinquish the world and renounce the false gods you serve. Jesus said to them, "Follow me, and I will make you fishers of men" (Matthew 4:19). Your false god can be your job, your house, your money, your car, your friends, and your drug or anything you idealize instead of serving the only true living God. Besides the Lord, there is no other God. He is who He is, Jesus, I AM. Think for a moment about the day you received salvation; you were a new Christian. You had an overflow of joy in your soul. You were running all over the place; you wanted to tell somebody about Jesus. The world cannot offer this kind of happiness, nor can the world take it away unless you allow. Redeem your joy in the Lord.

"Behold, all souls are mine; as the soul of the father, so also the soul of the son is mine: the soul that sins, it shall die" (Ezekiel 18:4).

"Dearly beloved, I beseech you as strangers and pilgrims, abstain from fleshly lusts, which war against the soul" (1 Peter 2:11).

I AM the Comforter

HEARING the Holy word of I AM is not always joyous when it requires a change in your attitude and behavior. According to Hebrews 4:12, "For the word of God is quick and powerful, and sharper than any two-edged sword, piercing even to the dividing asunder of soul and spirit, and of the joints and marrow, and is a discerner of the thoughts and intents of the heart." The Word of God is profound and revealed to those chosen only by God. Your shortcomings are noticeable when your character does not match with the Word of God. "But the Comforter, which is the Holy Ghost, whom the Father will send in my name, he shall teach you all things and bring all things to your remembrance, whatsoever I have said unto you" (John 14:26).

Your walk with Jesus is comforting when you look back over your life, and you see where He has brought you. You live in the world, but you are not of the world. You are not walking in sin and wickedness as before. Some people focus on having lots of money and power over others. How can you love Jesus and despise others? How can you love Jesus and wish harm on others? These things are not of God. Jesus Christ gave His life for all humanity. To all Christians, the world is a rest stop, but not your final resting place. Looking back will keep you back and looking ahead will keep you reaching for Jesus. Stay in prayer and walk in the power of the Lord.

Wherefore seeing we also are compassed about with so great a cloud of witnesses, let us lay aside every weight, and the sin that doth so easily beset us, and let us run with patience the race that is set before us. Hebrews 12:1

Dearly beloved, I beseech you as strangers and pilgrims, abstain from fleshly lusts, which war against the soul. 1 Peter 2:11

I AM Your Advocate

IN this world, you will never have justification from everybody. Justification means having a reason, having facts, circumstances, or a sound explanation in defense that something exists. In a court of law, regardless of the final decision, someone will always believe you are guilty when you are found innocent. "For all have sinned, and come short of the glory of God" (Roman 3:23). Jesus paid the price for our sins through His death. There is justification through Jesus Christ; He is our lawyer, jury, and judge. According to Romans 8:1, "There is therefore now no condemnation to them which are in Christ Jesus, who walk not after the flesh, but after the Spirit." In Hebrews 10:17, "And their sins and iniquities will I remember no more."

As a Christian, there will be times when you want to defend yourself for whatever reason. Hold your voice and let Jesus fight your battles. Let Jesus be your defense attorney. He knows the facts needed to support you properly. In 1 John 2:1-2, "My little children, these things write I unto you, that ye sin not. And if any man sins, we have an advocate with the Father, Jesus Christ the righteous." Jesus is the propitiation for the sins of the whole world. In Christ, you are justified and made free from the law of sin and death. You will go through tribulations so that Jesus can bring you out. The victory is in Christ, I AM.

"We know that whosoever is born of God sinneth not, but he that is begotten of God keepeth himself, and that wicked one toucheth him not" (1 John 5:18).

I AM Near

I T is not by accident that you were born. It is not by accident that you are reading this book. God does not make mistakes. Jesus had known you before you were born. He has a divine plan for you from the beginning of time. God created a masterpiece. When Jesus was on the cross, He saw a multitude of people. You were not physically standing at Golgotha, but Jesus knew your face, spirit, and DNA. He was aware of your present sin and future sin. And, Christ died for you on that old rugged cross. He died for everything that would be a challenge in your life. Jesus wrote your resume listing every celebration, revelation, laugh, tear, pain, and struggle you would have in life. He knew your destiny. Raise your hands high and bless God's name.

God is near, and there is nobody like Him. In Jeremiah 23:23, "Am I a God at hand, said the Lord, and not a God afar off?" The Spirit of I AM lives in you. Jesus is the forethought of God. Jesus answered Judas, not Iscariot, "If a man loves me, he will keep my words" (John 14:23). God's Spirit surpasses the evil in the world. Jesus does little, in a huge way.

Who hath saved us, and called us with a holy calling, not according to our works, but according to his own purpose and grace, which was given us in Christ Jesus before the world began.
2 Timothy 1:9

Jesus cried and said, "He that believeth on me, believeth not on me, but on him that sent me"
(John 12:44).

I AM Great Calm

A tropical cyclone becomes a hurricane when wind speeds reach more than 73 miles per hour. A hurricane's wind speed determines the strength of the storm: 74, 96, 111, 131, and 156 mph. A category five hurricane wind speed is 156 mph or greater. A level five is considered the most severe, causes catastrophic damage, sends debris flying, and causes coastal destruction. Deadly hurricane force winds are no match for Jesus. God created different storms: ice storm, blizzard, thunderstorm, snowstorm, hailstorm, windstorm, and tornadoes. He can bring great calm when high winds blow problems your way. In Mark 4:39, and he arose, and rebuked the wind, and said unto the sea, "Peace, be still." And the wind ceased, and there was a great calm. God's peace comforts you while the world is in chaos.

Unexpected conflicts on your job, in your life, in your marriage, and in your finances, can all be different storms. You are flooded with emotions while worrying about how you will tackle another disaster in your life: how you will pay one more bill, put gas in your car, buy grocery, raise the children, deal with mistrust, and handle another illness. How you will juggle life in general. Mayhem blows in doubt. The devil escalates the problem by planting seeds of desperation in your mind. He wants you to believe that Jesus does not care about you. In Romans 3:4, "God forbid: yea, let God be true, and every man a liar." Let Jesus plant seeds of tomorrow. You have to see yourself out of the storm. You will not be tossed about by high winds when you trust Jesus. Look to the Lord when you are unsure; He is your great calm.

"And when they were come into the ship, the wind ceased"
(Matthew 14:32).

I AM Living Water

JESUS grew weary while traveling to Samaria. Once He arrived in the city, He sat on Jacob's well to rest. At about the sixth hour, a Samaritan woman neared the well to draw water. Jesus said to her, "Give me to drink" (John 4:7). The woman pondered why Jesus, a Jew asked her a Samaritan woman to give Him a drink. Jesus being a great *discerner* knew her thoughts and everything about her life. He replied, "If thou knewest the gift of God, and who it is that said to thee, Give me to drink; thou wouldest have asked of him, and he would have given thee living water" (John 4:10). Jesus Christ is the living well that will never run dry.

In the last day during the feast of tabernacles which was a celebration that gave homage to the abundance of God's blessings. Jesus stood in the temple and cried, saying, "If any man thirst, let him come unto me, and drink. He that believeth on me, as the scripture hath said, out of his belly shall flow rivers of living water" (John 7:37-38). Because of His boisterous announcement, those knowing Jesus wondered why He was calling attention to Himself, especially when some sought to kill him. Jesus knew His time was not yet. Christ is extending an invitation to you today, come and drink the gift of life. If you believe Jesus, out of your belly shall flow rivers of living water. Jesus is everlasting life.

For by one Spirit are we were all baptized into one body, whether we be Jews or Gentiles, whether we be bond or free, and have been all made to drink into one Spirit. 1 Corinthians 12:13

"Whosoever drinks of this water shall thirst again, but whosoever drinks of the water that I shall give him shall never thirst; but the water that I give him shall be in him a well of water springing up into everlasting life" (John 4:13-14).

I AM Good News

YOU are watching a television program that is suddenly interrupted by music and big words moving across the television screen: BREAKING NEWS. "There is still time for *the lost* to accept Christ's invitation to receive eternal life." Bad news usually brings unrest. Good news brings joy. The gospel of Jesus Christ is good news. The news anchor reports that Jesus' death on the cross was for the atonement of man's sin. The reporter places emphasis on Christ's burial and resurrection. He ends the report with a direct message to the devil: Jesus is alive forever!

Jesus' death and resurrection were a triumphant victory for humanity. He is the glorious gift of eternal life, and His gift is free. You cannot die on the cross for your sins as Jesus. However, you have a cross to bear: live a holy life and die daily to sin. In Luke 9:23, "If any man will come after me, let him deny himself, and take up his cross daily, and follow me." Be a disciple of Christ by proclaiming His good works. Let your life be world-changing news to others that you are a follower of Jesus. Christ's love for you is unbreakable. There is no mountain high enough, no valley low enough—nothing can separate you from the love of God.

And we know that for those who love God all things work together for good, for those who are called according to his purpose. Romans 8:28

Nor height, nor depth, nor any other creature, shall be able to separate us from the love of God, which is in Christ Jesus our Lord. Romans 8:39

I AM the Salt

SALT is a mineral used to preserve food and slow down the decay of meat and food products. Salt enhances the taste of food. Salt can withstand high temperatures of up to 800 degrees Celsius. You will face many situations under extreme pressure. There will be many things you cannot change. Pressure is anger turned inside. Jesus knows your PSI (pressure per square inch in pipes) level. He gives you the endurance to manage explosive situations while waves of emotions attempt to control you. Jesus is the salt that preserves you. Stand strong in the Word. Jesus anointed His disciples to be the salt of the earth. They were ordinary men sent out amongst doubters to help spread the gospel. In retrospect, having received the anointing of Christ, you are the salt of the earth. Let your light shine that the world might see your works and glorify the name of Jesus.

As Disciples of Christ, you are salt in the midst of evil. There will be challenges trying to share the word of God. The ungodly will set traps for you. Be reminded that the world is dying from a lack of moral and spiritual guidance of their choosing. There are wars and rumors of wars. Christians are precious commodities set aside to house the Holy Spirit so the world will know God as the pure salt. Enhance the flavor in those around you by knowing just when to add a pinch of God's word. Do not lose your savor.

"Ye are the salt of the earth: but if salt have lost his savour, wherewith shall it be salted? It thenceforth good for nothing, but to be cast out, and to be trodden under foot of men" (Matthew 5:13).

I AM the Whole Armor

THE devil is on the prowl, seeking to change the mind of those who are on the verge of leaving the ways of the world. The devil's job is to keep you from becoming the salt of the earth and to bar the kingdom from entering you. Be sober and clear minded. Trust in the Lord and not in yourself. If you are not a child of God, then you are not equipped to fight the devil. You will not win by yourself. A wise soldier checks his gear and puts on his full armor before going to war. "Stand therefore, having your loins girt about with truth, and having on the breastplate of righteousness; and your feet shod with the preparation of the gospel of peace; above all, taking the shield of faith, wherewith ye shall be able to quench all the fiery darts of the wicked. And take the helmet of salvation, and the sword of the Spirit, which is the word of God" (Ephesians 6:14-17).

God does not put His armor on you and take it off again. Your spiritual armor is activated when you start each day with prayer and worship to God. Now, you are equipped to handle life's challenges in a productive way. You are clothed in Christ's righteousness and saved by His grace. In Romans 16:20, "And the God of peace shall bruise Satan under your feet shortly." The devil is no match for you when you wear the spiritual armor of God. The devil is no match for you when you have a made up mind to serve God. The devil is no match for you when he knows you love the Lord with all your heart. The devil knows you are equipped with the power of the Word to keep you. You shall live by the Word of truth. "Put on the whole armor of God" (Ephesians 6:11).

"Be sober, be vigilant; because your adversary the devil, as a roaring lion, walketh about, seeking whom he may devour" (1Peter 5:8).

I AM the Word of Truth

I AM God and the word of truth. If a man dies, he will live again. Those who Jesus makes free is free. "I am the way, the truth, and the life; no man cometh unto the Father, but by me" (John 14:6). Jesus is the truth, in Him is no unrighteousness. When the Spirit of truth comes, Christ will guide you in truth. God decided your outward features based on your assigned parents' chromosomes: your hair color, eye color, height, traits, and intelligence.

Your destiny is waiting. Jesus knew you would take some unadvised twists and turns along the way. It is okay because Jesus continues to direct your steps. The Spirit of Christ searches all things. The Spirit warns you and gives you a way out to avoid sinning willfully. When you go against God's warning, you grieve the Holy Spirit. The Spirit wants to guide you, and your mind wants to take another route. Jesus, the truth will never change. He can change you. Bless His name.

"Sanctify them through thy truth: thy word is truth" (John 17:17).

For I am the LORD: I will speak, and the word that I shall speak shall come to pass; it shall be no more prolonged: for in your days, O rebellious house, will I say the word, and will perform it, said the Lord GOD. Ezekiel 12:25

I AM the Ultimate Perfect Sacrifice

ARE you amazed when people go out of their way to obtain free things? I am. Think about Black Friday, the busiest shopping day of the year to kick off the holiday season. I am amazed at the time people get out of bed to be first in line to shop. Will you stand in line for Christ? Jesus freely offers salvation to all those who will accept Him as Lord and Savior. Jesus is certainly more valuable than gold, silver, rubies, pearls, and markdowns? Eternal life is a bonus—it is free with no hidden cost. The fine print tells you that His sacrifice for your sins comes with a no return guarantee. Jesus Christ, the ultimate perfect sacrifice, He paid the penalty for sin. Jesus is the only one who could connect man and deity.

The Lord is forever with you. Jesus hears your voice when you cry. God asks you to present yourself as a living sacrifice, holy unto Him. It is the sensible thing to do since Christ sacrificed His life for you. Do not act like the world: gloating in pride. Be governed by the Word. Jesus will not lead you astray. You have angelical bodyguards twenty-four hours a day. Jesus knows the exact time to close your eyes at night and open them each morning. He then waits for you to ask for guidance. He waits for you to claim each day as blessed and glorious in His name. Tell God you are dismissing your prearranged plans for the day and accepting His plans. He is ready to act on your behalf. Hallelujah to "the Great I AM."

I beseech you therefore, brethren, by the mercies of God, that ye present your bodies a living sacrifice, holy, acceptable unto God, which is your reasonable service. Romans 12:1

I AM the King of kings

THIS world has priests, rulers, presidents, lords, and kings, but Jesus comes to reclaim the lost. He is the "King of kings, and Lord of lords" (Revelation 19:16). In the last days, Jesus will pour out His Spirit on those young, old, male, female, wise, and unwise. The Holy Spirit fills believers who are baptized in the name of Jesus Christ, irrespective of one's culture, origin, or ethnicity. Jesus will pour out His spirit, causing His sons and daughters to prophesy; elderly men will dream dreams and young men will see visions.

Before Jesus returns to earth, dreams will be told, ideas will materialize, and the gift of prophecy will be spoken. The power of the Holy Spirit falls on His elect in unique ways. Now is the time to accept Jesus Christ as Lord and Savior. "Behold, he cometh with clouds, and every eye shall see him" (Revelation 1:7). What excuse will you have for rejecting Christ as the King of kings? The power from on high reveals those who truly love the Lord. In Romans 14:11, "For it is written, As I live, saith the Lord, every knee shall bow to me, and every tongue shall confess to God." I AM the King of kings.

For there is no respect of persons with God. Romans 2:11

And it shall come to pass afterward, that I will pour out my spirit upon all flesh; and your sons and your daughters shall prophesy, your old men shall dream dreams, your young men shall see visions. Joel 2:28

I AM Christ the Messiah

JESUS spoke with authority during His three-year ministry on earth. Christ [anointed] filled with the Holy Spirit and with power. Jesus Christ came on commission from God to save the lost. Jesus was a teacher, a healer, and much more. He performed miracles and cast out demons. Jesus spoke with compassion to His followers. He taught the true essence of love, forgiveness, mercy, faith, and hope. Daniel 4:3 says, "How great are his signs! And how mighty are his wonders! His kingdom is an everlasting kingdom, and his dominion is from generation to generation." Although Jesus is a conquering King, He came in no form or fashion. He preached to the lost and hurting; the crippled and blinded. He preached to all those that would hear and receive salvation.

Jesus did not come demanding honor and praise. In Luke 9:58, "And Jesus said unto him, Foxes have holes, and birds of the air have nests; but the Son of man hath not where to lay his head." The Roman rulers criticized Jesus for socializing with publicans and sinners. Jesus knew the mind of His haters and replied, "They that be whole need not a physician, but they that are sick" (Matthew 9:12). Jesus came as a humble servant. He went about teaching and preaching the Kingdom of Heaven to bring all sinners to repentance. "And I will put my spirit within you, and cause you to walk in my statutes, and ye shall keep my judgments, and do them" (Ezekiel 36:27).

Pilate, therefore, said unto him, Art thou a king then? Jesus answered, "Thou sayest that I am a king. To this end was I born, and for this cause came I into the world, that I should bear witness unto the truth. Everyone that is of the truth heareth my voice" (John 18:37).

I AM Your Anchor

AN anchor is a device used to keep boats in place or from drifting with currents. Gravity pulls currents downhill thereby reducing its potential energy to move the vessel. Emotions are similar to currents that move you. You will shift back and forth. At times you may be blindsided with problems that war against your flesh. Jesus is the anchor that keeps you from drifting into dangerous waters. If Jesus is not your anchor, the devil will be. The devil will annihilate anyone that is insecure and not washed in the blood of Jesus. If it were not for Jesus, you would drift from one person to another; and run from one worldly fix to another.

Furthermore, if you have achieved anything of worth, it did not happen because you are intelligent. You cannot luck into anything. It is the favor of God anchored in you by grace. And it is the destiny He planned for you. He illuminates your life. Stand up and show the world that Jesus saved you. Stand up and show the world that Jesus is a blessing. Jesus holds you in His hands. Stand up and tell the world that the Lord is your "Great I AM." People in the world are watching you, especially when you say you love the Lord. Let your conduct reflect the light inside of you. I AM, your anchor and the light of your soul.

"Let your light so shine before men, that they may see your good works, and glorify your Father which is in heaven" (Matthew 5:16).

Jesus answered, "Are there not twelve hours in the day? If any man walks in the day, he stumbleth not, because he seeth the light of this world" (John 11:9).

I AM Reason for Hope

THE world is perishing around you. People sense fear and unrest worrying about their future. Some people walk in ignorance while still refusing to acknowledge that Jesus Christ is real. Many are hopeless and feel lost. If you are someone who feels hopeless, come to Jesus, who is hope. He changes hopelessness into hopefulness. He is the same God who gave His life for you. The spirit of God is a mystery to those who walk in darkness. Jesus chose to take you who was hopeless, and show the world that He called you out of darkness, and into His marvelous light. Walk therefore in the hope of Christ's calling.

People who love the world will do the same thing as those in the world. You cannot do right unless Christ is leading you, and you are abiding in Him. Jesus is Holy, and He is asking you to be holy. Greater is Jesus Christ in you than he who is in the world. For this reason, "I am come that they might have life and that they might have it more abundantly" (John 10:10). I AM the way. I AM the truth. I AM life, and I AM your reason for hope. Hallowed be the name of Jesus forever and ever.

Who by him do believe in God, that raised him up from the dead, and gave him glory; that your faith and hope might be in God. 1 Peter 1:21

But sanctify the Lord God in your hearts: and be ready always to give an answer to every man that asketh you a reason of the hope that is in you with meekness and fear. 1 Peter 3:15

I AM Faith that Comes by Hearing

FOR those who love Jesus Christ, you know that His presence is with you. He waits for you to acknowledge Him and ask His will for you. Jesus sees far ahead of you. He knows the second, the minute, and the hour you encounter a situation that is too much for you to handle. He makes a way for you. God is a great Father, who loves you. He wants you to come to Him through faith and believe. Jesus wants you to come to Him for comfort and peace. Seek the Lord while He is near. He is proud of His children and waits with outstretched arms to welcome you home.

God's superior power holds everything in place, from the *Armillaria solidipes*, the largest living fungus in the universe that kills the root of trees to the smallest thing: the *singularity* located in the center of the black hole in space. Hear the word of the Lord and let it infuse your mind with unyielding faith that God is absolutely above everything. In Romans 10:9, "If thou shalt confess with thy mouth the Lord Jesus, and shalt believe in thine heart that God hath raised him from the dead, thou shalt be saved." Faith comes by hearing the Word of God. John 1:1 says, "In the beginning was the Word, and the Word was with God, and the Word was God." Having faith in the Word opens the windows of heaven. You are given access into grace through Jesus Christ.

And know ye this day: for I speak not with your children which have not known, and which have not seen the chastisement of the Lord your God, his greatness, his mighty hand, and his stretched out arm. Deuteronomy 11:2

Today if ye will hear His voice, harden not your hearts. Hebrews 4:7

I AM the LORD Your God

JESUS is Lord. He desires that you enjoy the life He has given you. Remember God's commandments said to Moses. You should have no other God before Him; take not the Lord's name in vain; keep the Sabbath day Holy; honor your father and mother; do not commit murder; do not commit adultery; do not steal; do not bear false witness; and do not covet. Keep these commandments and you will have rain in the middle of a drought. You will have peace in the mid of turmoil. You will walk in faith and not in fear. Your enemies will not harm you. The Lord establishes a covenant with you that He will be your God, and you are His child.

God is the Supreme Being, who is the standard to which the bar is set bringing everything under Him. He is I AM, the Lord your God. Jesus calls you out from among those who refuse to let go of the world. Have you ever wondered why Jesus called you? Have you felt a pull on your life to yield to His word? The worst criminal, killer, thief, liar, fornicator, and drug dealer can come to Jesus Christ, accept Him as Lord, and live a changed life dedicated to spreading the Word of God. Earthly fathers know their children. Jesus is your heavenly father and creator; He knows you. So, what is stopping you from having faith? In Galatians 3:13, "Christ hath redeemed us from the curse of the law, being made a curse for us: for it is written, Cursed is every one that hangeth on a tree." Jesus bore your sins on the cross. Bless the name of Jesus.

"If ye love me, keep my commandments" (John 14:15).

"If ye keep my commandments, ye shall abide in my love; even as I have kept my Father's commandments, and abide in his love" (John 15:10).

I AM All Access

IN the world, joining a club requires membership of some type. Some clubs cater only to elite groups of people. Club amenities are available to members only. However, obtaining membership is not always easy. You will pay astronomical fees to join and take an oath that you will follow club rules and dress codes. Club membership might depend on your wealth, place of residence, Ivy League college alumni status, or celebrity status.

Unlike the world, Jesus offers you access to eternal life in heaven. He is the door to the Kingdom. Jesus offers free membership to all that will accept Him as Lord and Savior. As an heir to the Kingdom, you will receive rights, benefits, and amenities free of charge. According to Revelation 22:17, "And let him that heareth say, Come. And let him that is athirst come. And whosoever will let him take the water of life freely." You do not need to have celebrity status in the world. Come educated or uneducated, homeless, sane, or with emotional baggage. Come rich or poor, although you will not need money in the Kingdom of God. You will leave sorrow, pain, sickness, and death behind. You will live in a mansion and walk on streets paved with gold. Accept the Lord's invitation to salvation and walk worthy of your vocation. Jesus holds your club card that gives you access to the amenities in heaven.

I, therefore, the prisoner of the Lord, beseech you that ye walk worthy of the vocation wherewith ye are called, with lowliness and meekness, with longsuffering, forbearing one another in love; endeavoring to keep the unity of the Spirits in the bond of peace. There is one body, and one Spirit, even as ye are called in one hope of your calling; one Lord, one faith, one baptism, one God and Father of all, who is above all, and through all, and in you all. Ephesians 4:1-6

I AM Increase

JESUS asks you to worship Him in spirit and truth. You persevere because you trust in Jesus, who the world does not know and understand. When you are faithful to a little, Jesus blesses you to have more. Christ will bless you, and He will bless your children throughout generations to come. In Deuteronomy 28:2, "And all these blessings shall come upon thee, and overtake thee if thou shalt hearken unto the voice of the Lord thy God."

Jesus speaks to you in different ways: directly, through visions, admonitions, scriptures, and through people. Jesus is absolute power, but gentle as a lamb. He is loving and full of peace and righteousness. Give heed to the voice of the Lord and obey him. "God judgeth the righteous, and God is angry with the wicked every day" (Psalm 7:11). Jesus is your increase.

Unto the church of God which is at Corinth, to them that are sanctified in Christ Jesus, called to be saints, with all that in every place call upon the name of Jesus Christ our Lord, both theirs and ours.
1 Corinthians 1:2

The LORD shall increase you more and more, you and your children. Psalm 115:14

I AM Forgiveness

B LESS the name of the Lord. All glory, praise, and honor belong to Him. Jesus is doing more for you than you can imagine. The depth of His love for you is immeasurable. He knows the magnitude of your sins. Jesus is perfect love. Romans 3:23 says, "For all have sinned and come short of the glory of God." You sometimes fall short and made mistakes. Can you say your heart is clean, and you are exempt from your sin? God forbid. There is no way you can justify your sins.

There is only one way--by His grace in which you have atonement. Jesus Christ paid the sacrifice at Calvary. His redemption frees you from the eternal bondage of sin. If you forgive your brother or sister who trespasses against you, then Jesus will also forgive you. If you do not forgive, neither will Jesus forgive you your trespasses. Jesus forgave you of all your sins. In Isaiah 43:25, "I, even I, am he that will blotteth out thy transgressions for mine own sake, and will not remember thy sins." Jesus, the epitome of Holiness and forgiveness.

Being justified freely by his grace through the redemption that is in Christ Jesus.
Romans 3:24

Who can say, I have made my heart clean, I am pure from my sin? Proverbs 20:9

"For if ye forgive men their trespasses, your Heavenly Father will also forgive you;
but if ye forgive not men their trespasses, neither will your Father forgive your
trespasses"
(Matthew 6:14-15).

I AM the Substance of Hope

FAITH is the substance of things hoped for and the evidence of things not seen. God has apportioned every man a measure of faith. If you have faith, and not doubt, you can say to the mountains in your life, go and be cast into the sea. Through Jesus, you have the power to speak to the problems in your life. Faith is having belief in Jesus who you cannot see. His Word asks you to believe, and you believe according to your measure of faith. God's word ignites your faith; the Word will thrust you forward to believe in things hoped for, the evidence of things unseen. Your faith is activated when you hear the Word of God. Do you believe Jesus exists because He changed you from inside out? If you answer yes, just watch Him take you further than you could ever imagine.

It pleases God when you exercise your faith. Do not think of yourself more highly than you ought to; be of a sober mind, based on the measure of faith allotted to you. What God has done for you, He can do for others. Be a prisoner of hope in good and happy times. Even when you are stubborn and argue with God, give Him the praise He deserves. The devil trembles when you walk by faith, trust Jesus to bring you victory over evil trying to come against you. Resist the devil and he will flee from you. Learn to speak the Word to your angels and watch things begin to shift in your life. Learn to lean on Jesus, and He will be your substance of hope.

For I say, through the grace given unto me, to every man that is among you, not to think of himself more highly than he ought to think; but to think soberly, according as God hath dealt to every man the measure of faith. Romans 12:3

I AM the Order of Your Steps

I AM the order of your steps. Jesus orders your steps in life. He will never lead you astray. He wants you to trust Him with all your mind and soul. The Lord will always give you a way out of every situation. You should not want for anything because God has everything ready, just ask Him. The Lord owns everything, even the cattle on the hill. He knows what you need and when you need it. If Jesus takes care of the birds—and He does—He will take care of you.

The Lord makes you lie down in green pastures by giving you rest. His angels watch over you when you sleep. He leads you beside still waters. He shields you in storms. He brings peace and serenity. Do not become angry when you hear news reports of the world. Do not become angry when you hear the world fighting about which political group is right or wrong. Jesus governs you and not the world. "The government shall be upon his shoulders; He is the Mighty God" (Isaiah 9:6). People have a tendency to trust the world and not trust Christ. You are right in step with your destiny. Keep your heart fixed on the Word, no matter what you see happening around you. You cannot see God, but God sees you, and He sees what is going on in the world. He is with you in spirit. He restores your soul and leads you to the path of righteousness for His name's sake. Through your agony and sorrow, Jesus orders your steps through His Word.

But my God shall supply all your need according to his riches in glory by Christ Jesus.
Philippians 4:19
Order my steps in thy word; and let not any iniquity have dominion over me. Psalm
119:133
O God, my heart is fixed; I will sing and give praise, even with my glory.
Psalm 108:1

I AM Your Shepherd

IN the beginning, God created heavens and the earth. The earth had no form; it was void and full of darkness. God said, "Let there be light" (Genesis 1:3). And God divided the light from darkness, and it was good. Though you walk through the valley of the shadow of death, you will fear no evil. Jesus is with you. He will give His angels care over you.

In this world, you will experience joy, sadness, and pain. But, through it all, according to Revelations 7:17, "God shall wipe away all tears from their eyes." Give Jesus your worries. He will take you through aches and sorrows. He will give you joy for tears. Everything the devil steals from you; the Lord will give back to you in good measure. Jesus is your shelter in turbulent times. Allow Christ to be "the Great I AM" in your life. His rod and staff will comfort you. Jesus shall never abandon you, even when the devil whispers, "Jesus does not care." The Lord prepares a table before you in front of your enemies. He will carry you through seen and unseen dangers. He anoints your head with oil. Your cup flows with blessings. God's goodness and mercy will follow you. Glory to Christ, I AM. Amen

"These things I have spoken unto you, that in me ye might have peace. In the world ye shall have tribulation: but be of good cheer; I have overcome the world" (John 16:33).

"Sanctify yourselves, therefore, and be ye holy: for I am the LORD your God" (Leviticus 20:7).

I AM Present Always

JESUS is an omnipotent God, who has the power to be everywhere at the same time. Jesus knows your thoughts before you speak. He knows the works of man and the intents of the heart. Christ knows that man desires praise for himself instead of giving Jesus praise and recognition. Many have deviated from God. A depraved mind that is void of God's Word yields to thoughts of evil, murder, adultery, sexual immoralities, lying, deceit, and blasphemies. These behaviors are opposite of Jesus Christ who is wisdom, love, grace, mercy, joy, salvation, comfort, peace, and faith. Jesus is pure and Holy. His love is perfect.

The world offers many beautiful, enticing things. Without the mind of Christ, you will fall prey and believe that this is a better way than accepting the salvation of the Lord. An old trick of the devil is to hit you at your weakest moment and cause you to believe that God does not exist. The devil is a master thief and liar. He disguises himself as good and caring. He wants you to rebel against Jesus. John 10:10 says, "The thief cometh not, but for to steal, and to kill." God comes so that you might have eternal life in Him. You must believe that Jesus is "the Great I AM" and He has worked things out for you. Just believe and call out His Word.

And we know that all things work together for good to them that love God, to them who are the called according to his purpose. Romans 8:28

I AM the Last Supper

AFTER Jesus had given thanks, He took the bread and broke it; He told His disciples that the breaking of bread represents His body. Jesus is the living bread that comes from Heaven. He who eats this bread will never die. The breaking of bread is in remembrance of the sacrifice Jesus made for you on the cross. In John 6:56, "He that eats my flesh and drinketh my blood, dwelleth in me, and I in him." Jesus then took the cup and gave thanks; He then passed the cup to His disciples asking them to drink. You must break bread with those who do not know Jesus Christ.

There is no remission of sin without the shedding of blood. While Jesus hung on the cross; a Roman soldier used his spear to pierce Jesus in His side: out came blood and water. Holy water fell to the ground giving life to those held captive in sin. Christ's Holy blood washed away sin giving them and everyone present and in the future the right to salvation and eternal life. Jesus will not drink of the vine again until He drinks new wine with you in the kingdom of Heaven. You are free from the shackles of sin. Christ died once and will never die again for the atonement of sin. Fear not, God is the first and the last.

"I am the living bread that came down from Heaven: if any man eats of this bread, he shall live forever: and the bread that I will give is my flesh, which I will give for the life of the world" (John 6:51).

And he took the cup, and gave thanks, and gave it to them, saying, "Drink ye all of it; For this is my blood of the new testament, which is shed for many for the remission of sins. But I say unto you, I will not drink henceforth of this fruit of the vine, until that day when I drink it new with you in my Father's kingdom" (Matthew 26:27-2).

I AM the Risen Savior

SILVER is a soft, white metal that is resistant to corrosion. Silver is high in monetary value. Many say that money is the root of evil. Judas Iscariot, one of the original twelve disciples, plotted with the chief priests and elders that he would help deliver Jesus Christ to them for thirty pieces of silver. Jesus was taken to Pontius Pilate, the Roman governor, and the judge presiding over Christ's trial. Judas did not realize the severity of betraying Christ until he learned that Jesus was sentenced to die. It was then that Judas felt remorse and attempted to return the money to the chief priests of the church. The elders refused to take the silver coins. The spirit of greed led Judas to betray Jesus Christ. Judas committed suicide by hanging himself.

Christ's death on the cross was horrific, although it was God's plan of salvation for the atonement of man's sin. In John 10:17, "Therefore doth my Father love me, because I lay down my life, that I might take it again." Salvation is to those who believe in the death and resurrection of Jesus Christ. In John 14:3, "If I go and prepare a place for you, I will come again, and receive you unto myself; that where I am, there ye may be also." The sacrifice Jesus made for you will never have a monetary value. And you can never repay Him. You cannot serve God and mammon [money]. You will love one and hate the other. You will hold to one and despise the other. There is nothing on earth more valuable than God's love for you. I AM is the risen Savior.

Then Judas, which had betrayed him, when he saw that he was condemned, repented himself, and brought again the thirty pieces of silver to the chief priests and elders. Saying, "I have sinned in that I have betrayed the innocent blood"
(Matthew 27:3-4).

I AM Yours Forever

GOD is aware of every move that you make throughout the day. He knows the intent of your thoughts before you speak. Jesus watches over you while you sleep at night. He is with you when you drive on dangerous highways. He is with you when you jog on dimly lit paths at night. He will keep your foes at bay and cheer with you in all your accomplishments. Jesus knows your pain and suffering. He knows that pain does not come without struggle. Your pain creates a special bond with Jesus.

Christ asks you to put your trust in Him rather than putting your trust in people. Christ holds the keys of the kingdom. He has prepared a place of rest for your soul. He is an awesome God, who loves you so much. Jesus was faithful to His Father, even while dying on the cross for the sins of the whole world. He is the author and finisher of your faith. In Hebrews 5:9, "And being made perfect, he became the author of eternal salvation unto all them that obey him." Obey God's commandments; be steadfast and unmovable. Greater is the faith of those who have not seen Jesus but believe in Him.

Then came the disciples to Jesus apart, and said, why could not we cast him out? And Jesus said unto them, "Because of your unbelief: for verily I say unto you, If ye have faith as a grain of mustard-seed, ye shall say unto this mountain, Remove hence to yonder place, and it shall remove; and nothing shall be impossible unto you" (Matthew 17:19-20).

The apostles said unto the Lord, "Increase our faith" (Luke 17:5).

I AM an Absolute Meticulous God

GOD was meticulous when He created the heavens and earth. God was meticulous in the creation of Adam and Eve. God was meticulous when He sent meat and manna from heaven to feed the Israelites in the Wilderness. God was meticulous when He gave the Israelites specific specifications to build the Ark of the Covenant. God was meticulous when He gave Noah specific dimensions to build the Ark. He was meticulous with the priests who entered the room of the Holy of Holies. God is meticulous with those chosen to preach the gospel. God is meticulous with those who will enter the kingdom.

God was meticulous when He chose craftsmen to build the temple. God was meticulous when He contemplated the temple's height, length, and décor. God was meticulous in selecting your purpose and destiny. God was meticulous with the timing of your birth and will be equally so with the timing of your death. He was meticulous in organizing the Bible--from Genesis to Revelation. God was meticulous when He selected the writers of the Four Gospels. God was meticulous when He chose the mother of Jesus and the road taken to redeem man from sin. The Lord is not the author of confusion. I AM, a meticulous God.

And God said, "Let us make man in our image, after our likeness: and let them have dominion over the fish of the sea, and over the fowl of the air, and over the cattle, and over all the earth, and over every creeping thing that creepeth upon the earth" (Genesis 1:26).

"Remember the former things of old: for I am God, and there is none else; I am God, and there is none like me" (Isaiah 46:9).

I AM Great Knowledge

A wise man seeks the wisdom of the Lord. Be careful that you are walking in the light and not in darkness. Satan is the Prince of Darkness and is given rule over unbelievers. Darkness is ignorance. Satan uses his power to infiltrate the mind of ignorance. He wants to harness your thoughts, ideas, aspirations, opinions, hopes, and beliefs. Satan desires influence in philosophy, government, education, and religion. Some nations are influenced by false teachings and idol worship due to the ideology of those in positions of leadership.

If you listen to the devil, you will wander aimlessly searching for what you think is truth. Lean not to your understanding. When you think you know, is when you do not know what is best for you. Many will perish for the lack of knowledge and understanding of God, Jesus Christ, and the Spirit. Words are a combination of thoughts. God spoke and created the whole world using words. When God speaks, you do not hear anything else, but His voice. He is a matter of fact, God. He is God with a plan that encompasses a beginning and an ending. In the beginning was *God, Word,* and *Spirit.* Jesus Christ [the Word] took on flesh and condemned sin in the flesh so you could become righteous. Jesus created light and became light. When a light is switched on, it pushes back the darkness. The devil has to back up when Jesus enters the house. Anyone that lacks knowledge let him ask God. The light will blind those who decide to walk in darkness.

In whom the god of this world hath blinded the minds of them which believe not. 2 Corinthians 4:4

"Now is the judgment of this world: now shall the prince of this world be cast out" (John 12: 31).

part 2

I am in the Great I AM

JESUS knew me in spirit before the foundation of the world. He is my Creator and Father. After the first Adam, I was spiritually dead and held hostage in sin without a right to appeal. I was a lost soul; an empty vessel with no sense of direction until one day I heard about a Savior named Jesus Christ. My life changed, and I have never been the same since believing in my heart, and confessing that Jesus Christ is Lord. I am in Jesus, and Jesus is in me. I have meaning and purpose in my life. God connects me to the head [Himself] of the body. I sit in Heavenly places in Christ; I AM.

My outward appearance resembles my earthly parents, but my inner being mirrors my Heavenly Father. Jesus is alive forever in me. I was once dead in sin until Jesus made me alive in Him. Jesus is a progressive God. His grace saves me each day. I am one body in Christ; the same as Jesus and His Father are one. "For as we have many members in one body, and all members have not the same office: so we, being many, are one body in Christ, and every one member, one of another" (Romans 12:4-5). I am blessed to be a member of the body of Christ, I AM.

Even when we were dead in sins, hath quickened us together with Christ, (by grace ye are saved); and have raised us up together, and made us sit together in heavenly places in Christ Jesus. Ephesians 2:5-6

But he that is joined unto the Lord is one spirit. 1 Corinthians 6:17

I am Restored in I AM

MY spirit resided in the midst of the valley of the dry bones, a rebellious sinner, and a wretch undone. I walked among thousands of other dry bones [the Israelites]. Thus said the Lord GOD unto these dry bones; "Behold, I will cause breath to enter into you, and ye shalt live" (Ezekiel 37:5). Jesus breathed the breath of life into my dry bones, and I became a living soul. "In him was life; and the life was the light of men" (John 1:4). His breath caused my dry bones to walk, to move, and to speak praises unto Him. I have authority to testify to other dry bones that Jesus lives. I AM restores me in hope, salvation, and love.

In Jesus, I received redemption, and everything that the Bible says belongs to me. I can do all things through Christ who strengthens me; He is my light and my salvation. He is my rock, my foundation, my deliverer, my today, and my tomorrow. Jesus holds my destiny. What the Lord has for me is for me, and no one can stop it from happening. I have gifts given to me from on high. I am blessed. Anything intended for evil; God will turn it around for good. I am restored to help spread the gospel of Christ to dry bones throughout the world.

Again he said unto me, "Prophesy upon these bones, and say unto them, O ye dry bones, hear the word of the LORD" (Ezekiel 37:4).

Blessed be the God and Father of our Lord Jesus Christ, who hath blessed us with all spiritual blessings in heavenly places in Christ: according as he hath chosen us in him before the foundation of the world, that we should be holy and without blame before him in love.
Ephesians 1:3-4

I am Strong in I AM

IT is a blessing to be a witness for Jesus Christ. It would be impossible to confess the Lord to others when I do not know Him myself. When opposition comes, I am reminded that greater is Jesus, who lives in me than the devil who rules from the air to those of this world. It is blessed assurance that Jesus is forever present in my life. It is with the mind of faith that I serve God. And faith through hearing the Word. Lord help me to resist temptation and to be secure in your perfect peace. Jesus conquered all sin and placed everything under my feet.

Christ's death on the cross manifest our bondage to sin is broken, and the order of creation connecting God and man is sealed. The devil trembles at the mention of Jesus' name. The devil knows he is no match for Christ. He cannot do one thing to me unless Jesus gives him permission. As was the prophet *Job*, who loved the Lord more than anything and anyone. *Job* manifested his love for God through worship and obedience, though he lost everything he owned. *Job* continued to praise God through all his turmoil. When praise goes up, blessings come down. God blessed Job more in his latter days than in his former days. "Finally, my brethren, be strong in the Lord, and in the power of his might" (Ephesians 6:10). Jesus, help me to be submissive to you and praise you in any circumstances. Thank you Jehovah-Elohim (Eternal Creator).

And the LORD said unto Satan, "Hast thou considered my servant Job, that there is none like him in the earth, a perfect and an upright man, one that feareth God, and escheweth evil?" (Job 1:8).

I am in the Glory of I AM

I am not without anything because God supplies all my need according to His riches in glory. When I asked Jesus to save me, I agreed to all the terms and conditions of salvation. I agreed to let Jesus rule and guide me in all things. I agreed to trust Him, accept healing by his stripes, and I agreed to His commandments. Where the Spirit of the Lord is, there is liberty. Shall I return to the entanglement of the world to be brought under the bondage of sin once again? God forbid. I have come this far by faith, and I know Jesus will never fail me. Jesus will never stop loving me.

Who is the King of glory? According to John 1:14, "And the Word was made flesh, and dwelt among us, (and we beheld his glory, the glory as of the only-begotten of the Father,) full of grace and truth." God gives His glory in fullness; we receive the whole God through salvation. His glory is mercy, strength, love, and His Holiness. "O Father, glorify thou me with thine own self, with the glory which I had with thee before the world was" (John 17:5). Christ is divine wonder and truth. What a wonder He is? "And then shall appear the sign of the Son of man in heaven: and then shall all the tribes of the earth mourn, and they shall see the Son of man coming in the clouds of heaven with power and great glory" (Matthew 24:30). Hallelujah to the glory of "the Great I AM."

"O Father, glorify thou me with thine own self, with the glory which I had with thee before the world was" (John 17:5).

Stand fast therefore in the liberty wherewith Christ hath made us free, and be not entangled again with the yoke of bondage. Galatians 5:1

I am Filled with the Spirit of I AM

THANK you, Lord, for filling me with your precious Holy Spirit. You are my eternal peace, comfort, and joy. Your Word fills me and keeps me still when I face difficulties. In my storms of life, Jesus brings calming words of assurance to let me know that He is here and that He will never leave me nor forsake me. You are Jehovah-Shalom (The Lord of Peace).

The Holy Spirit gives me power over the enemy to command the devil to flee from my mind. In Matthew 18:19, "That if two of you shall agree on earth as touching anything that they shall ask, it shall be done for them of my Father which is in heaven." As His child, I can call directly on the name of Jesus. The Word says signs shall follow those who believe. Christ says, "In my name shall they cast out devils; they shall speak with new tongues; they shall lay hands on the sick, and they shall recover" (Mark 16:17-18). According to Isaiah 54:17, "No weapon that is formed against thee shall prosper, and every tongue that shall rise against thee in judgment thou shalt condemn." Each day brings its challenges. I am thankful for the Spirit of the Lord.

How God anointed Jesus of Nazareth with the Holy Ghost and with power: who went about doing good, and healing all that were oppressed of the devil; for God was with him. Acts 10:38

This is the heritage of the servants of the LORD, and their righteousness is of me, saith the LORD. Isaiah 54:17

I am Complete in Christ I AM

I am complete in Jesus. Everything God creates is precise. Thank you for being a complete and absolute God. After Jesus had eaten the Last Supper with his disciples, He filled a basin with water and began washing their feet. When Jesus came to Peter, he asked whether He would wash his feet. Jesus responded, "If I wash you not, thou hast no part with me" (John 13:8). The washing of feet symbolizes Christ's love and humility. Jesus modeled servant leadership.

Although, there will be times when I have to shake the dust off my feet when people are unwilling to hear the Word of God. When Simon Peter understood why Jesus wanted to wash his feet, He said, "Lord, not my feet only, but also my hands and my head" (John 13:9). I am thankful to serve an absolute Holy God, who exemplifies compassion. I am grateful that the Lord washed me in love and compassion.

David, a man after God's own heart, worshiped the Lord through music, dance, and Psalms of praise. God anointed David to become the next king of Israel. Saul, the former King, grew jealous of David. His jealousy grew into hatred. David soon realized that the king he loved wanted to destroy him. David becomes a fugitive while trying to escape Saul's relentless pursue. He hid in a cave while running from Saul. God was David's shepherd who was with him in the valley of the shadow of death. When David had the chance to take Saul's life, he decided not to do so. David felt compassion for Saul. I am thankful for Jesus' compassion. He looks beyond my faults and sees my need for Him.

"If I then, your Lord and Master, have washed your feet; ye also ought to wash one another's feet. For I have given you an example, that ye should do as I have done to you" (John 13:14).

I am Pressing Toward the Calling in I AM

JESUS was the promised seed to come and redeem man lost in sin due to the spiritual death of Adam in the Garden of Eden. God was in the beginning, His word was in the beginning, the Word was with Him, and He was the Word. This mystery baffles those who do not know God; His plan of salvation established from the beginning of time. Jesus, the Son of God, was designated to restore the relationship between God the Father, and man. Jesus is the promised Messiah, my Savior. Jesus manifested in the flesh, justified in the Spirit, and is worshiped by His angels. Jesus healed thousands before going back to glory and now sits at the right hand of God. I press toward the goal in which Christ is calling. I press toward Christ when challenges engulf me. I press toward Christ when I face temptation. I have to press daily and hold firm to my faith in Christ. Thank you El-Elyon—the Highest Lord.

I press toward the mark for the prize of the high calling of God in Christ Jesus.
Philippians 3:14

Who hath saved us, and called us with a holy calling, not according to our works, but according to his purpose and grace, which was given us in Christ Jesus before the world began. But is now made manifest by the appearing of our Savior Jesus Christ, who hath abolished death, and hath brought life and immortality to light through the gospel.
2 Timothy 1:9-10

I am Thankful for I AM

DEATH was imminent with no way to escape the bondage of sin that leads to demise. But Jesus had a plan of salvation. His death opened a door of deliverance. I am glad the Lord paved the way for me to come to Him. He paid my debt of sin and secured my salvation by conquering demons and fallen angels. I am walking with Jesus. Lord, help me to enter your gates with thanksgiving and into your courts with praise.

I am thankful for those whom you have placed along my path as a source. I am thankful Lord, for your goodness and mercy all the days of my life. Help me to remember your presence each day. And, to be content in all situations, to be at peace with my neighbor, and to bless your name as God, the Father, even to those who do not know you. Thank you for a song in my heart and praise on my lips. Thank you Jehovah-Sabaoth--the Lord of Hosts.

I was glad when they said unto me, Let us go into the house of the Lord. Psalm 122:1

In everything give thanks: for this is the will of God in Christ Jesus concerning you. 1 Thessalonians 5:18

I am Seeds of Greatness in I AM

IN the book of Genesis, the very first chapter of the Bible tells how God spoke the earth and heavens in place. He separated water from water, and dry land appeared. Next, God seeded the dry land to grow beautiful plants, herbs, and trees. He called this orchard--The Garden of Eden. In all of its splendor, there was no one to tend the garden. So, God made man in His image. He named man, Adam. He was the first seed of greatness from God. Adam's job was to keep the garden, sow seeds, prune plants, and gather food from the garden for eating. God placed animals, and beast of all kinds, and creatures of their kind.

As an heir of Jesus Christ, I have seeds of greatness planted in me. The Word [seed] is planted in my heart. As the seed flourishes in my heart, I can spread seeds to those outside the harvest of God. I am a seed planted in the spirit of hope, abundance, success, endurance, love, forgiveness, meekness, joy, hope, peace, and seeds of faith. God says, "His seed remaineth in him, and he cannot sin because he is born of God" (1 John 3:9). I believe my purpose is to help plant seeds of greatness throughout the world to those who do not know Christ. Jesus is the true vine, strong, and mighty. He is Adonai-Jehovah--Lord our Sovereign.

Greater is he that is in you, than he that is in the world. 1 John 4:4

"And ye shall know the truth, and the truth shall make you free"
(John 8:32).

I am the Temple of God I AM

I am the temple of the living God. I was born of the Spirit in Christ Jesus. According to 1 Corinthians 3:16, "Know ye not that ye are the temple of God, and that the Spirit of God dwelleth in you?" To see the kingdom of God, you must be born again. The concept of being born again is a great mystery to those who do not know Jesus Christ. Nicodemus, a prominent Pharisee, and a member of the Sanhedrin ruling body of the Jews was baffled by the notion of rebirth. Nicodemus desired to understand how a man could be born again when he is old. Although, Nicodemus knew that a man could not enter his mother's womb a second time to experience a rebirth.

Jesus is the living water and Spirit of Life. The flesh is born of the flesh, and the spirit is born of the Spirit. The answer to Nicodemus' question of rebirth is that you must believe that Jesus died for your sins on Golgotha hill. Jesus told Nicodemus that a man must be born of water and the Spirit. Rebirth is a transformation of your beliefs. Rebirth is following the Word of God and yielding to the Spirit in obedience. Rebirth is walking no longer in sin but accepting the salvation of the Lord. In Romans 3:23, "For all have sinned, and come short of the glory of God." I am not my own. I am bought with the blood of Jesus.

What? Know ye not that your body is the temple of the Holy Ghost which is in you, which ye have of God, and ye are not your own? 1 Corinthians 6:19

Jesus answered and said unto him, "Verily, verily, I say unto thee; except a man be born again, he cannot see the kingdom of God" (John 3:3).

I am the Head and not the Tail in I AM

A football game begins when the captain of a team wins the call of either heads or tails. The team's captain then selects to receive the ball or kick the ball to the opposing team. In Jesus Christ, the notion of whether I have a life after death is not a game. In Christ, I am always guaranteed to land on heads and never on tails. The devil wants me to believe that I am playing from behind. Satan preys on those who have a double mind. Those who operate outside of Christ.

The devil wants me to bow and worship him and accept his lies. I serve an omniscience, God. Jesus is the first to return from the dead with all power over heavens and earth. Jesus set me free from the law of sin and death thereby sealing redemption and salvation with Him forever. I serve God, ruler of salvation. The head of all things. The Supreme God. Jesus drew me near when He rose from the dead. It does not matter if I am in the midst of chaos; Jesus says I am the head and not the tail. I trust the Lord, even when things are not going as I think. Jesus can take any bad situation and turn it around so that I can rise above it.

And the LORD shall make thee the head, and not the tail, and thou shalt be above only, and thou shalt not be beneath.
Deuteronomy 28:13

I am in the Rock, I AM

JESUS never promised me that life is a bed of beautiful roses without thorns. I will suffer great things for His name's sake. The Word of God prepares me to face fiery trials and tribulations. The closer I walk with Christ, the more persecution I experience and the greater I desire the peace of His presence. The scripture says I will suffer persecution for living godly. My help comes from the Lord, and my salvation rests on Jesus, the Rock. As stated in James 5:10, "Take, my brethren, the prophets, who have spoken in the name of the Lord, for an example of suffering affliction, and of patience."

Lord, give me endurance when sickness comes, and problems rush upon me without warning. Give me peace when rain falls with no end in sight; when winds blow from different parts of the earth and beat against the house that God builds. A house built on solid ground will stand. According to 2 Corinthians 5:1, "For we know that if our earthly house of this tabernacle were dissolved, we have a building of God, a house not made with hands, eternal in the heavens." A house built on sand will not stand. Rushing water will cause structural damage, and the house will fall. I will never have to worry if I let God build the house. Jesus is a solid rock.

"And the rain descended, and the floods came, and the winds blew, and beat upon that house; and it fell not: for it was founded upon a rock" (Matthew 7:25).

Yea, and all that will live godly in Christ Jesus shall suffer persecution. 2 Timothy 3:12

I am Bid to Come to I AM

JESUS told the parable of a king who invited many to His son's wedding feast. However, many sent regrets saying they could not come. The servants told the guests that their travel expenses are free, housing is free, and the table is ready. They refused the invitation again. When the king heard this, he told his servants, "Go ye therefore into the highways, and as many as ye shall find, bid to the marriage. So those servants went out into the highways, and gathered as many as they found, both good and bad, and the wedding was furnished with guests" (Matthew 22:9-10).

I have received an invitation to attend a grand wedding feast. The ceremony is in an elegant mansion located in a faraway land called Heaven. All expenses paid. I will feast on exquisite foods and delicacies prepared by the finest chef. I will see family and friends from long ago. I will meet people from near and far and learn we have much in common. The bridegroom is Jesus Christ, the Son of God. He is a conquering King and supreme God of heaven. Jesus paid a great sacrifice by shedding His blood for the remission of my sins. He is a glorious King, filled with grace, mercy, and hope. The Lord calls many, but few are chosen. Everybody has a calling, but few are willing to accept their calling from God who foreknew you before creation. Hear the voice of God. Will you reject Christ's bid to come to the wedding feast? All things are ready. Come go with me.

Again, he sent forth other servants, saying, "Tell them which are bidden, Behold, I have prepared my dinner: my oxen and my fatlings are killed, and all things are ready: come unto the marriage" (Matthew 22:4).

"For many are called, but few are chosen"
(Matthew 22:14).

I am Victorious in I AM

I was once the "poster child" of sinners. Now, I am victorious in Christ because of His death and resurrection. Jesus conquered every sin that could defeat me. As stated in 2 Timothy 1:7, "For God hath not given us the spirit of fear; but of power, and of love, and of a sound mind." He gives me permission to call upon His name, and He will answer. Jesus is a man of action. When Jesus speaks, things happen, things move, things appear, and the devil shudders. In Matthew 10:1, "And when he had called unto him his twelve disciples, he gave them power against unclean spirits, to cast them out, and to heal all manner of sickness and all manner of disease." Jesus empowered His disciples to carry the torch and let it burn brightly, the evil deeds of the wicked.

In trying times, Jesus is my perfect peace. I have power from the Word. Jesus gives me the authority to denounce evil in the world. The scripture encourages me to keep my mind on things above and not on things of the world. I am a victor and not a victim. Jesus, the Christ has given me everything I need to handle any challenge in life. Jesus proclaimed, "I am the resurrection, and the life: he that believeth in me, though he were dead, yet shall he live" (John 11:25). The Apostle Paul wrote that he was willing, "To be absent from the body, and to be present with the Lord" (2 Corinthians 5:8). It is a joy to know that the body is a temporary house, and God's spirit dwells deep within the soul. 1 Corinthians 15:55 states, "O death, where is thy sting? O grave, where is thy victory?"

Finally, brethren, whatsoever things are true, whatsoever things are honest, whatsoever things are just, whatsoever things are pure, whatsoever things are lovely, whatsoever things are of good report; if there be any virtue, and if there be any praise, think on these things. Philippians 4:8

I am in the Hands of I AM

A ND Christ went a little farther, and fell on his face, and prayed, saying, "O my Father, if it be possible, let this cup pass from me: nevertheless not as I will, but as thou wilt" (Matthew 26:39). Jesus detested the shame of the cross, but at the will of his Father, He took on the weight of our sin. Christ's sacrificial death broke the yoke of sin. Isaiah 10:27 states, "It shall come to pass in that day, that his burden shall be taken away from off thy shoulder, and his yoke from off thy neck, and the yoke shall be destroyed because of the anointing." I am forgiven and washed in the blood of Jesus. I am no longer yoked to sin but in the mighty hands of I AM.

According to the book of Romans 6:13, "Neither yield your members as instruments of unrighteousness unto sin: but yield yourselves unto God, as those that are alive from the dead, and your members as instruments of righteousness unto God." The righteousness of Jesus sets me free from sin. If the righteous barely make it in, where will the wicked and sinners appear? The devil cannot enter into a spirit-filled house and spoil its goods unless I allow him to take control of the house. God forbid, I am in the Mighty hands of the Lord. Glory to "the Great I AM."

And if the righteous scarcely be saved, where shall the ungodly and the sinner appear? 1 Peter 4:18

"No man can enter into a strong man's house, and spoil his goods, except he will first bind the strong man; and then he will spoil his house" (Mark 3:27).

I am Sanctified in I AM

THE devil is a master manipulator. He tries to disguise himself as an angel of light while planting deception that Jesus is an imaginary figure. He wants me to believe that the Bible is a lie. The devil represents all forms of evil. He is the father of lies. The word of God is wiser and stronger than any trickery of devil. The devil is no match for Jesus. He knows that Jesus holds all power in His hands. The devil knows that Jesus sits high and looks down at his evil deeds. Satan knows that it is a matter of time before Jesus annihilates him and those who serve him. He knows that his time is ending, and Christ is coming soon for all to see that He is the absolute superior God. Jesus will never again be led through halls to answer the rulers of this world. He will never again be spit on and mocked by the ungodly. He will never be hung again on an old rugged cross. But, Christ will return as the glorified conquering King.

In Romans 14:11, "For it is written, as I live, said the Lord, every knee shall bow to me, and every tongue shall confess to God." All will give an account to God for their deeds. I am waiting for Christ's return. I serve a mighty God, who can do abundantly more than I can imagine. God spoke, and the power of His Word created the world; on the sixth day He created man, and on the seventh day He put his feet up to rest. I bow before my Lord and Savior. He is Lord, and His plan of salvation goes forth each day. Christ sanctified me by faith. I worship Him in spirit and truth. Hallelujah to Jehovah Nissi—the Lord our Banner.

"To open their eyes, and to turn them from darkness to light, and from the power of Satan unto God, that they may receive forgiveness of sins, and inheritance among them which are sanctified by faith that is in me" (Acts 26:18).

I am Rooted in I AM

THROUGH the mercy and grace of God, I am firmly rooted in Christ. In Psalm 1:3, "And he shall be like a tree planted by the rivers of water, that bringeth forth his fruit in his season; his leaf also shall not wither, and whatsoever he doeth shall prosper." I am rooted in Christ, and I shall not be moved. His Word is planted deep within me. The spirit of God connects me to the vine; my lifeline to Jesus. I am substance created in truth and love. Jesus is the way, the truth, and life.

I am growing by faith and overflowing with thankfulness for what Jesus has done for me. I am grateful that my present and future is in Him. I am not what I was when Christ rescued me out of darkness. I am blessed with favor each day from the Lord. I am thankful that Jesus wakes me up at the right moment each day. He is the Potter, and I am the clay. Please, Lord, keep fashioning me into the beautiful vessel you want me to be. Thank you for fighting battles that I am not able to fight. You are the head of my life and my counselor. Help me, Jesus, to never forget to pray for others and give you the praise.

Open to me the gates of righteousness: I will go into them, and I will praise the LORD: this gate of the LORD, into which the righteous shall enter. I will praise thee: for thou, hast heard me, and art become my salvation. Psalm 118:19-21

Rooted and built up in him, and stablished in the faith, as ye have been taught, abounding therein with thanksgiving. Colossians 2:7

I am a Living Sacrifice in I AM

THE mind is in a constant battle against the attacks of the devil. The voice of the wicked wants to control my thoughts and behavior. The mind wars against deception from the devil. Greater is Christ Jesus, who is a mighty conqueror. The Word says to gird the loins of the mind; to be ready; to be sober; to have eternal hope for the grace given by Christ. The strength of my faith hinges on my trust in God. I must have continuing faith as my God is immense. "For we wrestle not against flesh and blood, but against principalities, against powers, against the rulers of darkness of this world, and against spiritual wickedness in high *places*" (Ephesians 6:12).

The Spirit fills me with love. By His mercy, I present my body as a living sacrifice. I must die daily to sin. Jesus Christ is the propitiation for our sins in prayer. Jesus sacrificed His life for the sins of the whole world. "I beseech you, therefore, brethren, by the mercies of God, that ye present your bodies a living sacrifice, holy, acceptable unto God, which is your reasonable service" (Romans 12:1). I am holy because Jesus is Holy. The wisdom of the world is foolishness to God. I have a moderate understanding of what is good, acceptable, and the perfect *will* of the Father. Thank you Jehovah-Hoseenu—the Lord our Maker.

Wherefore gird up the loins of your mind, be sober and hope to the end for the grace that is to be brought unto you at the revelation of Jesus Christ. 1 Peter 1:13

I am Taught by I AM

JESUS is a master teacher; He taught the multitude in parables based on heavenly concepts illustrating moral truths in simple everyday language. Christ's teachings glorified the Father. These parables emphasized principles on compassion, love, mercy, strength, healing, faith, and forgiveness. Believers understand the parables and how to apply them in everyday life. But to those who refuse to hear are lost, and confused by the parables. I am thankful for the discernment of God's Word.

Jesus told the parable of a man paralyzed from birth who believed that one day He would be able to walk. Jesus told the parable of the Mustard Seed; the Good Samaritan; the Hidden Treasure; and the New Wine. Jesus told the story about the Ten Virgins; the Rich man and Lazarus; the Vine and Branches; the Bread of Life; and the Prodigal Son. During His three-year ministry on earth, thousands of followers were healed and delivered from demonic spirits by faith while hearing Christ's teachings. Many heard the Word [the Parable of the Sower] and allowed the Word to fall among thorns. Thereby the hearer becomes unthankful and unfruitful. Let's be a reader, hearer and doer of God's Word, thus having our lamps filled with the anointing Spirit of God.

"And Jesus, when he came out, saw much people, and was moved with compassion toward them because they were as sheep not having a shepherd: and he began to teach them many things" (Mark 6:34).

"But he that received seed into the good ground is he that heareth the word, and understandeth it; which also beareth fruit, and bringeth forth, some an hundredfold, some sixty, some thirty" (Matthew 13:23).

I am Power of Authority From I AM

THE popularity of Jesus quickly spread throughout regions when people heard how He cast out evil spirits; cured a man of leprosy, healed a sick woman with a blood disease; fed five thousand people with two fish and five loaves of bread, and how He walked on water. Yes, many wanted a free meal, and others genuinely desired salvation. When I first heard about Jesus, I tried to run as fast as I could away from God. I wanted to stay just as I was in the world. My life was good, and I did not need to change. But one day, the Word took hold of me and my life has never been the same. Silver, gold, money or fame cannot take the place of Jesus.

Christ gives me the power of attorney to ask for anything in His name. I have the anointing of the Holy Spirit to lay hands on the sick, and to cast out demons. I have power over my enemies through Christ. Jesus stated in John 14:12, "Verily, verily, I say unto you, He that believeth on me, the works that I do, shall he also do, and greater works than these shall he do; because I go unto my Father." I have the authority to come boldly to the throne of Grace and ask the Father whatsoever in the name of Jesus. Glory to the power of I AM.

Then said Pilate unto him, "Speakest thou not unto me? Knowest thou not that I have the power to crucify thee, and have the power to release thee?' Jesus answered, Thou couldest have no power at all against me, except it were given thee from above: therefore, he that delivered me unto thee hath the greater sin" (John 19:10-11).

"And in that day, ye shall ask me nothing. Verily, verily, I say unto you, whatsoever ye shall ask the Father in my name, he will give it you"
(John 16:23).

I am Redeemed in I AM

I am redeemed in I AM. There is no reason for people to be ignorant of who Jesus Christ is and what He did for humanity. The Word of God is talked about and preached on television, on YouTube, CDs, in books, movies, and in every source of social media. Mercy on those who are still trying to get their life in order before confessing Jesus is Lord. The archangel of God will announce the second coming of Jesus Christ. Those dead in Christ will rise first. Those who are alive will rise to the clouds to meet the Lord.

As Christians, we patiently wait for the return of Jesus. There is only one Lord, one faith, and one baptism. The same Spirit that enabled Jesus to rise from the dead lives in us. He will quicken our earthly bodies by His Spirit. According to Matthew 24:40-42, "Then shall two be in the field, the one shall be taken, and the other left. Two women shall be grinding at the mill; the one shall be taken, and the other left. Watch therefore: for ye know not what hour your Lord doth come." Dear Lord, have Mercy on the one left behind; that one will weep in sorrow. I AM is my redeemer. El-Olam— the Everlasting God.

And Jesus said, "I am: and ye shall see the Son of man sitting on the right hand of power, and coming in the clouds of heaven"
(Mark 14:62).

For the Lord Himself shall descend from Heaven with a shout, with the voice of the archangel, and with the trump of God: and the dead in Christ shall rise first: Then we which are alive and remain shall be caught up together with them in the clouds, to meet the Lord in the air: and so shall we ever be with the Lord. 1 Thessalonians 4:16-17

I am in Godly Love--I AM

I am thankful for the Holy Spirit, who is "the Great I AM." I am grateful for Godly love that has no boundaries. I am thankful for Christians whose heart overflows with His love. Charity being the greatest gift of all. Brother Paul stated elegantly, "And though I have the gift of prophecy and understand all mysteries and all knowledge; and though I have all faith so that I could remove mountains, and have not charity, I am nothing" (1Corinthians 13:2). Thank you, Jesus, that I am nothing without charity. Lord, help me to walk in charity.

I am grateful for Christ's love and the plans He has set in motion for me. I was stubborn and disobedient, but thanks be to God for giving me a renewed mind and heart aligned with His spirit and not of the flesh. I am so grateful for His mercy. There is no other love greater than the love of Jesus. His love is longsuffering and humbling. His love empowers me to mount up with wings like an eagle so that I can soar high, although I may get weary. Jesus is my help. I know that trouble will come, but it is for God's Glory. I am persuaded that nothing can separate me from God. Godly love is Christ's faithfulness and unconditional love for humanity. Thank you, Father.

Keep yourselves in the love of God, looking for the mercy of our Lord Jesus Christ unto eternal life. Jude 1:21

But they that wait upon the LORD shall renew their strength; they shall mount up with wings as eagles; they shall run, and not be weary, and they shall walk, and not faint. Isaiah 40:31

I am in the Power of I AM

I am in the power of I AM. God spoke the world into existence. His Word created beautiful mountains, oceans, and landscapes. God created man whom He gave authority over everything that talks, walks, and crawls on earth. I am in the power of I AM. I am a member of the body of Christ. Every promise spoken by God, He keeps. His divine power has given me everything I need in life. His godliness helps me to understand who He is. God has given me the power to escape poverty and disease. The power is in the Word.

I give reverence to Jesus, who was with me when I experienced a close call with death. His love and the warmth of His presence was with me in a cold hospital room. I had lost a significant quantity of blood. The world was in panic mode over the AIDs virus. Jesus purified the blood transfusion needed by this earthly body to function. Although, I know it was the divine flow of Christ's blood that gave me salvation. During another point in time, Jesus was with me when I received a diagnosis of cancer from a new physician. The Lord ordered my steps to seek another diagnosis. The devil tried to destroy me, but Christ's grace and mercy would not let me go. My tribulations were for the glory of God. The other physicians found no signs of cancer. God's love is supreme. Hallelujah! I am a chosen heir of God. I can come boldly to the throne of grace. If Jesus has done anything for you, as He has for me, join me and be a witness of His power.

Praise you the LORD. Praise God in his sanctuary: praise him in the firmament of his power. Praise him for his mighty acts; praise him according to his excellent greatness. Psalm 150:1

Let us therefore come boldly unto the throne of grace; that we may obtain mercy, and find grace to help in time of need. Hebrews 4:16

I am Walking in the Spirit of I AM

GOD had known me before I knew myself. I am living the life He designed for me before the world was created. I believe a part of God's plan was that I sat under the teachings of the Pentecostal church. When I was a baby, the intensity of my cry determined whether I was sick or hungry. The fulfillment of my needs depended on my parents. When I was a baby Christian, my diet consisted of milk and soft food. I had to learn to walk in the Word.

The Word is everywhere you want to be. I lived in Japan for a few years, after returning home, I registered for college to combine the courses I took while living out of the U. S. I was also, an active member of the church. After a few classes, I bought a set of encyclopedias. I was offered a gift with the purchase. I chose a series of Biblical books--Genesis to Revelation. I began using the reference books immediately, while the other books set neatly on a shelf. However, seeing them every day, I felt drawn to them. One day I picked up the book of Genesis. I found myself spending hours reading and meditating on the stories written. I sensed a closer relationship developing with Jesus. He started speaking to me in the spirit more and more. The more I read, the more I enjoyed His presence and wisdom. I learned that God would hold nothing from you. Jesus baptized me with fire from on high as He had baptized many on the day of Pentecost in the book of *Acts*. I have not apprehended. I remain dependent on my Father, "the Great I AM."

> *"And let him that is athirst come, and whosoever will, let him take the water of life freely"* (Revelation 22:17).
> *"And, behold, I send the promise of my Father upon you: but tarry ye in the city of Jerusalem, until ye be endued with power from on high"* (Luke 24:49).

I am in God, Jesus Christ, and Holy Spirit: I AM

GOD, Jesus Christ, and the Holy Spirit are one in peace, holiness, love, and Sovereignty. God's name is I AM. The Spirit dares you to embark on a journey of discovering your identity in Him. I encourage you to know that your purpose and destiny lie in the greatest gift ever given to humanity: Jesus, the Christ. He is my Lord. Your beliefs are generated in your mind, which is where change begins.

Study the Bible for yourself to understand how God, Jesus Christ, and the Holy Spirit connect as one Spirit. Jesus is the perfect love that fills the void in our lives. No one or nothing can fill my soul as Jesus can. Jesus is perfect, and virtuous. All the money in the world will not make my life complete as Jesus can. Only the *Word* will transform you into the temple of God. If change is what you desire, then believe the Bible is true. I am who the Bible says I am, I can do what the Bible says I can do, and I have what the Bible says I have. According to 1 Peter 1:23, "Being born again, not of corruptible seed, but of incorruptible, by the word of God, which liveth and abideth for ever." I was buried with Jesus and resurrected with Jesus. He is the Word that is incorruptible and eternal.

But the word of the Lord endureth forever, and this is the word which by the gospel is preached unto you. 1 Peter 1:25

"It is the spirit that quickeneth; the flesh profiteth nothing: the words that I speak unto you, they are a spirit, and they are life" (John 6:63).

I am Who I am in the Great I AM

WHEN Adam ate the forbidden fruit in the Old Testament, the ground was cursed for his disobedience. Henceforth, the earth would bring forth thorns and thistles. In the New Testament, a crown made of thorns and thistles was placed on Christ's head to mock Him as king of the Jews, and to degrade the notion of Him as God, the Messiah. In the Old Testament, a young unblemished ram caught in a thicket was offered as a burnt offering in place of Isaac; the son promised to Abraham from God. In the New Testament, Jesus the unblemished Lamb of God shed His precious blood for the remission of man's sin. The blood of Jesus is a cleansing agent for sin, it still speaks, it still calls, and the blood will never lose its power.

The nails in Christ's hands and feet supported the weight of our sin, nailing sin to the cross, thereby breaking the curse of sin. My hands are to worship and lay on the sick, and they shall recover. His blood orders my steps. A Roman soldier speared Christ in the side, blood, and water gushed out onto the ground. The water baptized those dead in Christ. His blood changed my image, I see God instead of seeing me. His blood delivered me from the power of darkness. "But he was wounded for our transgressions; he was bruised for our iniquities; the chastisement of our peace was upon him; and with his stripes, we are healed" (Isaiah 53:5). Out of my mouth, I will glorify Him as God forever. His grace for us was not in vain. I am not yet fully who I will become, but by the Grace of God, I am who I am in I AM.

"I said therefore unto you, that ye shall die in your sins: for if ye believe not that I am he, ye shall die in your sins" (John 8:24).

Psalm 23

The LORD is my shepherd; I shall not want.
He makes me lie down in green pastures: he leadeth me
beside the still waters. He restoreth my soul:
he leads me in the paths of righteousness for his name's sake.
Yea, though I walk through the valley of the shadow of death,
I will fear no evil:
for thou art with me; thy rod and thy staff they comfort me.
Thou preparest a table before me in the presence
of mine enemies:
thou anointest my head with oil; my cup runneth over.
Surely goodness and mercy shall follow me all the days of my life:
and I will dwell in the house of the LORD forever.
Amen

"My Father, which gave them me, is greater than all; and no man is able to pluck them out of my Father's hand. I and my Father are one" (John 10: 29-30).

CONCLUSION

IN the book of Exodus, Moses asked God what name he should tell the sons of Israel. God replied, "*I AM who I AM. Tell them I AM sent you.*" *I AM God the Father, Jesus Christ, the Son, and the Holy Spirit.* When you confess that Jesus Christ is Lord and Savior, the Word takes root in your heart. You will transition from depending on the world to depending on God. You will understand that God is the creator and that you are created to serve Him with all your heart.

God is absolute. He is a progressive God. The presence of His peace is with you always. There will be growing pains and challenges being a new Christian. But, you know maturity comes as you study the Word. God says, "The words that I speak unto you; they are spirit, and they are life" (John 6:63). You begin to understand who *I AM* is, and that there is no other God besides Him.

You must understand the power of speaking 'I am' to the giants in your life. I have learned that prayer is powerful, and it is important to pray. And, I understand the power of speaking *I am*, and not just talking, thinking, wishing, and dreaming about changes in my life. I am asking you to speak by faith to your Goliath. Jesus gives you authority to use His name. You have to believe and not doubt that what you say will happen. The words you speak have power, so, do not speak negative things into your life. Do not say I am never going to be able to get better or I am never going to have peace.

I am asking you to be a prisoner of hope and expect change. Things may not happen immediately, but when you speak in the name of Jesus, His power sets things in motion. A group of attorneys goes to work after hearing your situation; they build your defense by gathering information, collecting evidence, speaking to witnesses, and searching laws related to your case to be equipped to argue your defense.

So, activate your faith by speaking *I am* to bring you victory and not defeat. You can begin by saying, "I am blessed with skills, talents, and wisdom. I have the ability and the power to do all things through Christ who strengthens me. Every demonic plague against my family or me is broken in this generation and generations to come, in Jesus name."

"I am blessed to lend, and not borrow."

"I am blessed with health and strength."

"I am a child of God."

"I am sanctified in the Lord."

"I am above and not beneath." I believe if you speak, using *I am* in faith, you will see amazing things happen in your life. I believe God will bless you to prosper in every area of your life. You and your family are blessed, even in difficult times. Jesus says in John 16:33, "These things have I spoken unto you, that in me ye might have peace. In the world ye shall have tribulation: but be of good cheer; I have overcome the world."

The devil is the adversary of Jesus Christ. The devil will tell you that God is a Biblical figure. He will try to entice you with the riches of this world, if only you worship him. Always remember that things come with a price. If you serve the devil, your reward is spending your life in eternal judgment. God reigns with supreme power. I AM is your *Jehovah Jira*: your provider. Trust and believe in *I AM* and watch as your life transition from the inside out.

God, Jesus Christ, and the Holy Spirit is "the Great I AM."

He is the Rock; his work is perfect: for all his ways are judgment: a God of truth and without iniquity, just and right is he. Deuteronomy 32:4

"I am the bread of life. He that cometh to me shall never hunger, and he that believeth on me shall never thirst" (John 6:35).

"I am the vine, ye are the branches: He that abides in me, and I in him, the same bringeth forth much fruit: for without me ye can do nothing" (John 15:5).

"I am the resurrection, and the life: he that believeth in me, though he were dead, yet shall he live: and whosoever liveth and believeth in me shall never die. Believest thou this?" (John 11:25-26).

"I am the good shepherd: the good shepherd giveth his life for the sheep" (John 10:11).

"I told you, and ye believed not; the works that I do in my Father's name, they bear witness of me. But ye believe not, because ye are not of my sheep, as I said unto you. My sheep hear my voice, and I know them, and they follow me" (John 10:25).

"And there are three that bear witness in earth, the Spirit, and the water, and the blood: and these three agree in one" (1 John 5:8).

ACKNOWLEDGEMENTS

I acknowledge my colleagues and fellow authors in Scribblers & Scribes, and Heartland Authormixx who shares the passion of writing. As you know, writing is not an easy task. Thank you for compassion and support. To my dear friend Bailyn Grey, a skillful and passionate writer. Thank you for positive encouragement. And to Pam Spears, who never fails to make me laugh out loud.

I acknowledge Lynn Heacock and JoLynne Crout-Deuel for taking time out of their busy schedule to read the script in its initial stages. I give acknowledgment to Carla Rice, my friend, and mentor. To Cindy Wester for her ingenious way with grammar. You are a woman of substance and a role model to many who know and do not know Jesus Christ. I acknowledge Tammy Dennis for your supportive spirit. God blessed you with a gift of artistic talent and creativity to make something ordinary into something extraordinary. I acknowledge Anna Genoese, who is a gifted editor and Ted Bowman: author of Get Published without Getting Ripped Off. Thank you!

I give reverence to Jesus Christ, my Savior--without him, I am nothing.
Thank you for opening doors. You are Mercy, Grace, and my
'Great I Am.'

About the Author

DEBRA Thompson is the author of The Crumb Snatchers. She was born is Cleveland, Mississippi, and lives in Central Florida with her husband, Earl. She earned a BA and MA in education from the University of South Florida. Debra enjoys sports, travel, fishing, and walking on the beach. Her passion is writing, reading, and spending time with God. Debra is the mother of three children: Cory, Rachel, and Elizabeth Thompson. She has two beautiful grandchildren: Jasmine Danielle Thompson-Hamilton and Carter Earl Thompson-Hamilton. And, son-in-law: Lawrence Hamilton. Debra is a member of Scribblers and Scribes, the Florida Writer's Association, Heartland Cultural Alliance, South Florida Writers Association, and the president of Heartland Authormixx.

.